WONDERBOY

WONDERBOY

and The Life & Times of
Drewford Alabama

JAMIE MORRISON

SEREN

Seren is the book imprint of
Poetry Wales Press Ltd
Suite 6, 4 Derwen Road, Bridgend,
Wales, CF31 1LH

www.serenbooks.com
Follow us on social media @SerenBooks

ISBN: 978-1-78172-765-2
Ebook: 978-1-78172-770-6

A CIP record for this title is available from the British Library.

The publisher acknowledges the financial assistance of the
Books Council of Wales.

Cover illustration: Pete Fowler.

Printed by Bell & Bain Ltd, Glasgow.

This is a work of fiction. All of the characters, organisations,
and events portrayed in this novel are either products of the
author's imagination or are used fictitiously.

This book is dedicated to Oriana.

The year – 2005

Location – London

Mood – Dramatic

My eyelids slowly part. I'm waking up on a cold, hard, unforgiving floor. As I start to get used to no longer being unconscious, I begin to scan the darkened room. I see a sink, pots, pans, a stove. I'm lying on someone's kitchen floor, one which I certainly don't recognise.

As I begin to coax myself up, I quickly discover that I'm surrounded by smashed wine bottles and dried claret – claret in the cockney sense: blood.

It's at this moment a tremendously awful pain begins to rush from my left hand. On further examination I discover the hand in question is stuck in the fist position, like a boxer, the dried blood acting like superglue. By the amount of red on and around me I imagine that this clenched position most likely stopped me from bleeding to death whilst I was out for the count. Forcing open my hand in the darkened kitchen brings a jolt of laser-type pain through my whole body. I'm greeted with a nasty gash, the wound running from my middle finger all the way to the start of my wrist.

I'm now obviously wide awake. The damaged hand explains the blood, the events leading up to the wound are still a mystery, although I imagine the broken bottles are the likely culprits.

I pick myself up with no idea what happened, where I am, or where I've been – an all too frequent predicament.

Hold on!

Let me stop here.

Unaware of where I am.

Surrounded by glass, covered in blood. WOUNDED!

This isn't an ideal first impression of who I am, in fact I would say, like, not at all. Taking a bird's eye view of the situation, I can confidently say that before this point this type of behaviour wasn't how I saw my life going in the slightest.

Let me not get ahead of myself though as I want to discuss the butterfly effect. The particular analogical theory that a butterfly flapping its wings in Richmond Park, London could trigger a hurricane on the other side of the world. That's not true of course, the intended sentiment is how the smallest of moves can lead to the most colossal outcomes. It's like a set of dominos positioned side by side, the tiniest push setting them all toppling in a constant series of events caused by a single action.

This is what happened to me. I couldn't stop my dominos from falling.

It's what you would call fate. Why I'm here today is a mixture of hard work, coincidence, and luck or what some may call a very hard to comprehend '*nah that couldn't have happened*' series of events.

Although the real reason I start my story here is a literary device, something recently taught to me. It's all about juxtaposition, salt and sweet, hot and cold, just like my favourite dessert, a delicious freshly baked apple pie with a big scoop of ice cream. And why am I telling my story in the first place? That's simple. All good stories must be told and most importantly, I promised someone I would. You will meet them soon.

PART ONE

The years – 1980s

Subject – Wonderboy

Location – Sleepy Oak, Surrey, UK

My name is Pop! Pop Morrison. I am the Wonderboy. I was christened Andrew Reese Morris by my parents, Verity and Clarence, but at no time in my life do I recall being called Andrew. It's been Pop since day dot. I'd never thought much about how my snappy name came about; it's just always been that way.

I recently asked Mum over tea and biscuits why I was called Pop, and her response was rather brilliant.

"When you were born you just popped out. It was like you couldn't wait to get out there and make a racket."

I changed my second name to Morrison when I was eighteen because of my favourite rock and roll singer Jim Morrison from The Doors. I thought Pop and Morrison together had a great ring to it. I also knew I needed a good name if I was going to be a famous musician, and at that age those were the stars I was aiming for.

I was born in Guy's Hospital, London and grew up west of the big smoke in the leafy green Surrey countryside, a little nook of a village with no streetlights called Sleepy Oak. Sleepy Oak is a one road in, two roads out type of place, with a small pub, The Cricket Club, and a very old red telephone box which would eventually be converted into a tiny library homing mostly romantic literature or books about gardening.

Our family home was called The Old Rectory and was named on account of, one, its age and two, because it was located right next to the church. Mum had the place done just right; it was shabby chic before shabby chic became a thing. I loved the long weeping willow-lined gravel drive: the satisfying raspy crunch walking to or from was the most comforting sound. The whole place was wondrous, growing up there was a treat.

The name Sleepy Oak comes from the huge oak tree that grows on a steep bank that sits by the road at the main entrance to the village. This 'sleepy oak' leans precariously low to the ground, almost as if it's trying to lie down – horses, motorcycles, cars, and most vans can successfully enter Sleepy Oak this way. The drive under the tree is always a thrill for those who don't do it daily, a novelty almost. Anything bigger in size, a removal lorry for example, has to take the back entrance to the village, a slight detour, certainly the less glamorous arrival to the village but equally as effective, and hence my odd 'one road in, two roads out' description. Many visitors comment on the tree saying it's dangerous as it will fall one day. It hasn't yet, and I don't think it ever will.

I believe its roots go deeper than any opinion.

Family life was pretty carefree, no qualms here, my parents were top notch. Mum was a history teacher until she retired and became a semi-professional yoga instructor and Dad once worked from home as a business manager, something involving looking after other people's money. I'm an only child. Apparently after I 'popped out' the idea of having another one of me was rather unappealing to my folks, during the same tea and biscuits chat Mum's exact words were, "You were a bloody handful, love!"

I never once thought that being an only child was a bad thing: to me it always meant that I just got extra brilliant Christmas presents.

Before POP was even part of my vocabulary, before I even had any vocabulary for that matter, my grandparents on my mother's side moved to Sleepy Oak. I never met my grandparents on my Dad's side as he was adopted, and as soon as he came of age he bounced and never looked back. Grandma and Grandpa Robins fast became my best friends. The constant buzz of excitement surrounding their lives was something I always wanted to be around. My grand-folks lived in a thatched cottage across the road opposite our house. It was a beaten-up old place when they first bought it, abused and derelict. They always laughed about when they first went to see the property and how there was a cow in the living room and frogs in the bath. Pretty quickly they put the love into the house that it needed. They even started the garden from scratch. Apparently I 'helped out' by planting flowers. Sadly, I was too young to remember that although I certainly loved watching the garden grow as I did.

To me it felt like a magical place.

I must add that my grandparents' surname 'Robin' was not official, not from birth or marriage. They would become 'Robin' on account of the bird variety that lived in abundance on their Sleepy Oak grounds. Their cottage was ideal for many reasons, the main one being that there was ample space in the back garden to build an observatory, something they of course needed as they were both astronomers.

Grandpa and Grandma Robin's journey to become husband and wife is a rather beautiful story. They first met as kids when they were both sent to the same summer camp in Edinburgh, Scotland, a land they were both born and raised in. Due to their high IQ they were both considered to be 'the odd ones out'. It would seem their soaring intellects were a rare statistic amongst the other summer camp kids; something that would turn out to serve them well as being considered 'odd' would be the exact nucleus needed to draw the two together. It was simple: they became friends, best friends, sweethearts then boyfriend and girlfriend. You see the trajectory, right? Like a rocket ship into space. Well sadly this fairytale ended when they both went to different universities in different countries to study the very same subject. Astronomy. Life went on and time passed, but because of their astronomic passions as young adults they naturally ended up moving in the same professional circles, this being the spark that would eventually bring the two star-crossed lovers back together again. That, and something rather celestial.

What inspired their rekindled love was Grandma discovering a new constellation. This was a big deal made bigger when she would go on to name it Jym. Spelling the constellation Jym was of course considered a pretty big signal to my future Grandfather whose name and unique spelling was identical. As they were both now working at the Royal Observatory in Greenwich, Jym wasted no time in asking Jane out for a steak dinner, and the rest, as they say, is history.

Grandpa Jym never reached the same heights of astronomical successes as Grandma. He always said that he was much more content being Grandma's 'right hand man in work, and partner in crime in love.' He became far more interested in clouds, anyway, studying them rigorously in his spare time to the point where he became a professor on the subject. Their skyward obsessions were incredibly inspiring to me, and even as a small boy I knew their passion for their professions was extra special. This unwavering commitment planted a seed in my young mind. It was duly noted that in later life I should feel the exact same way about my job as Grandma and Grandpa did about theirs. During the never-ending school summer holidays, I would camp out by the observatory for weeks at a time in a bright orange tent next to a gnarly apple tree, with a rope swing wide enough for two. I will never forget how that tree produced the biggest apples you ever saw.

During these summer holiday evenings Grandma would let me look through her elite science grade telescope and teach me all the names of the planets and constellations. Of course, I would always ask to see constellation Jym and she would always gladly oblige.

Eventually these evening telescope sessions would result in Grandma playfully quizzing me on all the galactic names.

"What's this one called Pop?"

Sadly, I didn't fare well with this game, unless it was Jym that is. I really didn't mind, I just enjoyed spending time with her. I believe that's exactly how she felt too. My skyward quizzes didn't stop there though as spending time with Grandpa would always result with him pointing up to the heavens. As an officially knighted specialist in the great subject of clouds Grandpa went on to teach me all the variations of the fluffy sky pillows, and for reasons beyond me, this information stuck like gum on a shoe. There's ten, you know. They all have cool names like Cirrus or Stratus. My favourite was always Nimbus and Mammatus. I just love the way they both rolled off the tongue. Grandpa adored the Cirrus variety. He called them 'good luck clouds.'

"If you see them good things are coming," he'd say.

Jym and Jane were not your typical grandparents by any stretch of the imagination. For one they loved everything that was going on in the sky above them far more than what was happening on the ground below. Except me, of course, who was doted upon and thoroughly indulged.

It's highly controversial, but along with astronomy and cloud names they also taught me very early on about the immense healing abilities possessed by someone they both were very fond of called Mary Jane. Well, it didn't take me long to work out for myself that this 'Mary' was not a person at all, but a plant. 'Mary Jane' of course being marijuana. It seems every generation has a new name for this psychoactive bush, my personal favourite being Wacky Baccy, or just the good old classic 'grass.'

When Grandma and Grandpa moved to Sleepy Oak, they began growing the Ganja plants in their greenhouse-esque observatory to the great dismay of my parents who would eventually just have to ignore this penchant their elders had for pot.

This curious Wonderboy couldn't help asking questions, which of course they always happily answered. Incidentally it was my Grandpa who gave me the Wonderboy nickname.

I remember the exact day. It was my tenth birthday, late morning. I was riding my brand-new red mongoose BMX bike around my grandparents' garden when this small blackbird startled me causing a minor crash. I knew this bird well. For some reason it had been stalking me, I mean literally ever since I could remember. Every time I cared to look there had always been a small blackbird in my general vicinity, observing me. Eventually I just took it for gospel that wherever I went it would be there. I even thought this happened to everyone, but of course this wasn't the case, and after many years I got so used to its presence I stopped acknowledging it altogether. To be totally honest I even ended up naming it. I began calling this bird Albee. Albee the small blackbird. I figured the creature needed a name, and Albee felt right.

Albee the bird never bothered me or made me feel uncomfortable. If anything, he just made an already curious boy wonder.

As Grandpa helped me and my BMX off the ground, I asked him the reason why a small blackbird followed me around everywhere I went. Grandpa told me it was like a guardian angel.

"Not all Wonderboys and girls have them, but you're special Pop. He's there to look out for you and you alone."

I asked Mum and Dad this same question later that day. Their answer was simple and far less wondrous: Coincidence!

The thing is, I had already done enough private observing of my feathered friend to know this wasn't coincidence at all. What Grandpa told me only solidified that.

At some point in my early teens, whilst taking part in our night-time stargazing tradition, Grandma started to let me take a puff or two from her perfectly rolled joints. I never looked back. It didn't take long, but once I learnt how to roll for myself, me and my friend Carmen would secretly sneak into the observatory to smoke a cheeky doobie: the secrecy aspect of this ending when a plate of cookies started to magically appear halfway through our doobie, 'anonymously' appearing on the doorstep after a selection of spritely knocks on the observatory door.

Carmen was my first girlfriend. She didn't go to the same school as me, but lived in the next village along, a 15-minute walk on the road or a 5-minute walk through farmer Pierce's corn field and across a babbling brook on precarious stepping-stones. She would later move away when her dad got a job in America. We stayed in touch via letters and occasional phone calls until one day they just stopped. My first heartbreak? Well, that's how I described what I was feeling in my diary!

(Diary extract)

Why does thinking about Carmen make me sad? Is this what the films call heartbreak? Dad told me that there's plenty of fish in the sea. I told him I don't care about the other fish in the sea, I liked that one. He said one day I will understand. I've been waiting a while.

This diary was one of my first, and it was Grandpa who encouraged me to keep one. I enjoyed taking a moment to reflect. I liked the idea I could be reminded of things in the future, feelings, moments, observations. I always loved this particular diary: it was covered in fake fur and had a little lock and key, both useless as I discovered a paperclip and bit of force were just as effective as a means of access.

As a kid I ran an absolute riot in the academia department. 'I' and 'it' just never clicked. Looking back at it all now, school was just simply not for me. This I appreciate is odd considering I was coming from such an academic family, but no, not the case at all, much the opposite. I was a constant nuisance in class – an incorrigible little terror whose class clown antics nearly got me expelled many times over. The 'very nearly' bullet dodging made possible only by my Dad working his tactical magic with Mr Atkins the head teacher.

Nice one Dad!

This was the trouble-making flight path I was on; that is, until something rather tremendous happened. I was skipping gym class, something I always did, which would inadvertently bring me face to face with my destiny. I must say out of all the school lessons, I hated sports with a particular passion. For me the only redeeming feature about it was wearing football boots. I just loved the sound of the metal studs against concrete floor – the satisfyingly percussive clippaty clappaty got me every time. It was the whole sporty part of it all that I loathed. I was an overweight kid and absolutely detested the locker room atmos. Getting changed into my gym kit was an arduous task to say the least. Mum and Dad would always say that I would 'lean out' when I got older, but that information didn't help me one bit back then. I was the only fat kid in class, and you can only imagine all the comments.

Hey fatso!

Oi, look at chunky.

Boys will be boys, right?

I felt like I was the same as them, but clearly, I wasn't. Fortunately for me, it was only ever the locker room where I got any type of grief, but grief is grief no matter where it's applied.

The ring leaders of my locker room torment were the Christie twins who took great pleasure in causing distress to others. To this day I can still hear their squeaky pre-pubescent venom-laced voices. The tipping point for me was the time they hid my clothes after cricket practice, forcing me to leave the locker room to get help or refuge in just my underwear. When I returned with the no-messing-around Mr Peters, my clothes were back where I'd left them, the twins were gone and the rest of my classmates sheepish and silent. Mr Peters with his stupid raised eyebrow looked at me like I was seeking attention, like I made the whole thing up.

FUCK THAT, I thought. I vowed to never ever go back again.

I hated the Christies, and I hated the locker room hierarchy. I retired from physical education that day. A self-imposed honourable discharge on the grounds of emotional distress. So, while skipping sports class for the above reasons, I would find myself walking past the school's music department and right into my destiny-defining moment. I never usually went that way to bunk off, far too much opportunity to cross paths with teachers and their subsequent instant detention hand-outs. That day for some reason I was unconcerned with such issues. There I was on my way with great intention to cause some sort of tomfoolery with the other school misfits. It's really not hard to get labelled with that naughty schoolboy credential. You'd better believe, though, I was thoroughly committed to keeping mine fully maintained and up to date. All this disobedience melted away the moment I walked past the semi soundproof windows at the back of the music block. What I heard was a sound I instantly wanted to know more about. Scrap that, I *needed* to know. It was just like tasting chocolate for the first time. There was no going back from that first sugary hit, I would always need more. You see at the back of the music department there was a row of shoebox size practice rooms, just enough space for one-to-one music lessons. Every day a different instrument would be taught by a series of professional musicians who would visit the school. Monday was brass, Tuesday strings, Wednesday singing, Thursday guitar and Friday, the very day I was skipping swimming lessons to smoke cigarettes and write swear words on school property was DRUMS. La Batterie, Tympana, Trommel…

DRUMS, DRUMS, DRUMS!

For a moment I stopped dead in my tracks. After this initial stun faded, I moved closer to where the glorious noise was emanating from. It's then when I looked through the thick glass window and saw inside the little room a youngish man – The Teacher, I presumed, just absolutely wailing away on a drum kit. He looked like a man possessed and I knew that this was the most exciting thing I had ever witnessed in my life. I was totally transfixed, completely and utterly mesmerised. Every time he hit those shiny cymbals and sparkly drums my fascination grew with further intensity. I identified with what I was seeing instantly. The whole aesthetic look of the instrument spoke to me in a language I didn't even know I could understand.

It's hard to describe, but what I was seeing made complete sense to me. I immediately connected in a way I had never connected to anything before. I could feel this was a big moment, the biggest moment, bigger than chocolate.

I was a 14-year-old kid who suddenly knew exactly what I wanted to do with the rest of my life.

I wanted to be a drummer.

There was no doubt about it, a drummer is what I was going to be. This overweight rebel kid balancing on his tip toes, nose pressed up to window would forever be spellbound by what he had just witnessed. From that moment on, there was no more naughty rebellious Pop. I became more of what you would call, a precocious Pop. I had no time for that school silliness anymore; it was all about the drum life for me now.

Straight away I signed up for lessons and took the money I earned from mowing peoples' lawns in Sleepy Oak to buy myself a drum kit. I was already cutting my parents' and grandparents' grass which I loved doing – to me there's something very therapeutic about it. I also get the same thing with hoovering and organising cupboards. Back then Dad said if I branched out further afield with my grass cutting skills, i.e. cutting the neighbours' lawns and charging for the effort I could make a little pocket money for my troubles. And that's exactly what I did. I was a young man sitting pretty on 255 quid, I remember feeling distinctly like I was a millionaire. It was also most fortunate for me that the 5-piece oyster pearl drum set I had seen sitting majestically in the local music store window was exactly £250.

That was it. My first domino piece began to fall.

This was my first truly memorable encounter with fate. I even had enough left over to buy some ear plugs and a big bar of chocolate – it was Cadbury's fruit and nut, delicious. Unfortunately for me I wish I'd worn the ear plugs more. One word: tinnitus.

Only two years later, another fate-like epiphany would hit me with the same force.

I was sixteen years of age, just old enough to be left home alone, so when my parents departed for a summer holiday somewhere sunny and tropical, I immediately set up my drum kit in the family living room directly in front of the television. That summer, the box was permanently tuned in to one of the two music channels available, and I would happily sit there behind my drums for hours upon hours playing along to all the music videos from the popular bands of the day.

I started to notice that I didn't look like any of my favourite drummers. I couldn't pinpoint it at first, but it slowly dawned on me that all of my drum heroes were skinny where I was not. It was like the school locker room all over again. I felt like I was the same as them until I realised I had this one major weighty flaw.

This hit me hard. It felt like I was doomed to fail before I even got going, not because my love, desire or commitment wasn't fiery enough, oh no. Because I was overweight.

It was a daft realisation, but in my mind, I wouldn't stand a chance of 'making it' if I was the way I was: FAT.

I began to care about my size. Previously I hated being called 'chunky,' although this word was never enough for me to curb my eating. My MTV realisation was different though: it's what you would call 'defining' as nothing else would be more important to me than reaching my goal of being a world-famous drummer. There was no sacrifice too big or small which I would allow to get in my way.

(Diary extract)

I heard in school from one of my teachers that becoming a famous drummer is almost impossible for a troublemaker like me. They said it's the equivalent of winning the lottery. I told Grandma this. She told me the very word 'impossible' says I'm Possible.

That's all I needed to hear. I am now running every single day. It's as important as my drumming practice. I've just knocked a 6th hole into my Marks and Spencer belt. I now know it is not impossible to lose weight if you put your mind to it.

I am excited and confident about my future. There's now nothing in my way. I've taken a further step to being an adult. I can feel my training wheels are off. I am heading to a destination unknown. Happy days.

If adulthood was being compared to an uncontrollable rollercoaster ride you could say I was strapped in, ready for take-off, good or bad!

The year – 1994

Mood – Rhythmic

Occasion – Self Discovery

I'd been fully consumed since that fateful day behind the school music block. I was a rhythmically enthusiastic boy, turned into a drum-obsessed man. The obsession brought with it a religiously meticulous practice and exercise routine, which over time translated nicely into the early rumblings of a potentially successful drumming career which I could see clearly bubbling away on the horizon. I exemplified what it was to be a hungry ambitious musician. I was eighteen years old and officially Pop Morrison. Making way for my new all-encompassing rhythmic religion, I moved out all non-drum related furniture from my bedroom.

Bed, desk, wardrobe gone. Drums, drums, drums in.

I proudly stuck posters of all my favourite drummers on my walls: tub thumpers like Buddy Rich or my first celeb crush, the beautiful Miss Sheila E from Prince's band. Even Animal from the Muppets had a spot on my bedroom wall. It was something about his reckless wildness which caught my impressionable attention.

Every night I slept on a fold out mattress in a sleeping bag right next to my drum set. I did this so my beloved cylindrical beacons of sound could be the first thing I saw each morning and the last thing I saw at night.

Obsession and crazy do go hand in hand.

At some point after all this practice and diligence something changed within me: something *'just clicked'* in my mind and every time I sat behind my kit I began moving with the drums in ways I had never done before, my body almost dancing around to whatever beat my hands were playing, weaving and flowing in and around the rhythm in a way that just seemed to make complete sense to me, my movements and expressions helping me feel closer to the music and feel the sonic vibrations stronger and stronger, and I now knew I was well on my way to learning about the true meaning of **PURE VIBES**.

"Looks like Pop could be onto something," I overheard Mum say to one of her friends. Mamma Pop was of course talking about my drumming! You see, besides causing a ruckus in school and never forgetting a face, cloud, or a good story, I'd never really been particularly great at anything before. With drums, I really was. I'd been practising up to ten hours a day from the moment I didn't have school getting in the way and subsequently I was getting rather good.

It turns out I had a natural ability for hitting things.

My drum teacher even said, "You make those drums sing Pop."

I had the holy grail of drumming assets – *feel*.

There was no doubt about it, the drums were bringing out the best in me and just like my grandparents, I was doing exactly what I was supposed to be doing with my life.

Every weekend I would get the train to London and head straight to Denmark Street or 'Tin Pan Alley' as it was known in the 50s. Even back then, this little central London street was already considered a mythical place, a real hub for musicians and songwriters. For the longest time every single store on the small road was music related, with a warren of record labels, management offices, and radio stations. Like a drumming yo-yo, I would spend the whole afternoon walking up and down, taking it all in, its past and present glories, hoping my presence would absorb some of the magic musical juju.

I went into all the shops and introduced myself to fellow musicians and sonic adventurers. My hobby for chat was in its early stages but the mutual subject of music always got the ball rolling.

One day I was talking to Tommy, the owner of what was considered the best drum shop in London. Tommy was in his mid-60s and had been selling drums on Denmark Street for 35 years. Eventually he clocked that I visited his store every Saturday. He could sense I was keen and obliged with feeding my enthusiasm and curiosity by sharing his vast knowledge of rhythm, obscure drum tuning techniques, and stories of selling drums to the world's greatest drumming legends, from Karen Carpenter to Ginger Baker.

I was enamoured and I went back there to learn more every weekend.

It went like that for a long time until, one Saturday, Tommy announced to me and a handful of shoppers,

"Pop if you're gonna be here every weekend you may as well be getting paid for it."

That was it. Tommy gave me my first ever job in the music business and from then on, every weekend I went to Tommy's to hang out with all the drums and got paid for the privilege. I made teas, coffees, unpacked new stock and sometimes helped the customers.

The best was when famous drummers stopped by. Tommy had a wall reserved for celebrity musicians' signatures. I will never forget the day Alan White, the Oasis drummer came in to try out some vintage snare drums. I asked him to sign my arm – I didn't wash for at least two weeks. Eventually Mum stencilled it on to a drum skin and had it framed for me.

It was a blissful time, looking back it felt like a nostalgic never-ending summer, like a perfect movie montage of MEGA.

Pretty soon I had passed my driving test, and instead of just weekends I would begin to head into London every night of the week visiting jam sessions in the back rooms of old boozers, or singer-songwriter nights anywhere across the big bustling city.

My mission? I was on the hunt for absolutely anyone who needed a drummer.

I had thousands of business cards printed up, which I would relentlessly hand out to anyone who seemed to care.

Every day I would leave home with two handfuls, and I wouldn't return until I had given every last one of them away.

I knew something would come from these cards. I also knew I only needed one of them to connect. You see with that one moment of connective opportunity I knew that there was no way I couldn't turn it into two opportunities, then three, then four, then who knows where? I knew with crystal-like clarity that this was how it was all going to start. To me it felt like I had the winning numbers for the lottery in my back pocket. I felt like I was truly destined to succeed, no ego, no arrogance, just pure self-belief.

To understand what my definition of success was, was easy. All I wanted was to play drums every day for anyone who wanted me, and I mean anyone. As long as I was given enough money to pay for my fuel and buy a cheese sandwich at the end of the day, I was all yours. I was the definition of a cheap date, the musical sideman of your dreams. My goals would eventually change as goals have a habit of doing, but back then that was it, pure and simple.

My business cards along with my visible excitement and obvious ability worked a treat because in a relatively short period of time I was gaining lots of attention and getting constant requests to come and play music. At a certain point I even stopped having to hand out my cards as the best business card there was began to take over. Word of mouth. Apparently, I still have boxes of the cards in my old bedroom at Sleepy Oak. They really are hilarious.

FOR ALL YOUR DRUMMING NEEDS
CALL POP MORRISON

This was before I had a mobile telephone, so the Sleepy Oak home number was given, often a caller would be greeted by Mamma or Papa Pop who would write down on a little stickie pad of paper who called, what style of music they played, and when and where they needed me.

My folks would leave these notes stuck to the fridge door for me to see when I got back home from my day of musical adventuring, and right after I ransacked the fridge for leftovers or cake, I would peruse the colourful sticky notes containing my future job opportunities.

It was always exciting to see what was waiting for me and it was a rare day that the Morrison family fridge was sticker-less with new musical possibilities.

The next morning, I enthusiastically accepted each opportunity. 'NO' back then was what I considered forbidden vocabulary. I somehow instinctively understood that playing with as many people as possible, in as many styles as possible, would be a big part in how I was going to become a world-famous drummer. All I had to do was play, play, play so it was always, YES, YES, YES.

One day, as I was getting ready to leave Sleepy Oak for the big smoke, I received a different type of phone call, a new type of proposition that would go on to change everything.

This wasn't the standard call to play for a singer-songwriter or someone needing me to fill in for a drummer gone missing in action.

Nope, this was different.

This was a permanent type of call.

I was asked to join a band.

"You will be in a real band, involved in all aspects of the group's affairs," the American manager lady said. She went on, "The band consists of a male and female busking duo."

The duo was spotted by the American lady whilst they were busking Jimi Hendrix cover songs in Piccadilly Circus.

The lady said, "I've been working with them for a month. It's time to replace Piccadilly Circus for more traditional venues. They need to leave the streets and to do this they need a drummer. Not just any drummer, a drummer with 'spirit and fire,' and I believe that's YOU Pop!"

She told me that my style had been duly noted, and there was no one else out there who suited the position more perfectly.

I said yes without thought or hesitation and, after arranging to meet up in an old crusty rehearsal room underneath a railway arch in Shepherd's Bush, I thanked the lady and politely asked what her name was. She had of course introduced herself at the start of the call, it's just her proposition had induced the audio equivalent of tunnel vision. What can I say? I was riddled with excitement.

"My name's Cynthia Andrews," she said. "I saw you playing at the Jazz Cafe in Camden. I got your business card from the venue after the show."

I knew it! I thought smugly to myself. I knew it would all start with my hysterical business cards.

After a little small talk, I thanked her again, wished her a good day and then hung up the telephone.

Seconds later I was shouting up to my mum who was at the other end of the house.

"MUM I'M IN A BAND!"

"WHAT YOU CALLED?" she shouted back.

"THE SOHO'S. WE'RE GOING TO BE MASSIVE."

Mamma Pop responded with her only ever request for my day-to-day London adventures.

"YOU DRIVE SAFELY NOW POP."

"WILL DO MUM," I shouted back, oblivious to her concern.

The Wonderboy, in under a handful of years, had created a buzz in and about town as the new young drummer to watch out for.

Every night, I was out there covering all styles of music from jazz, rock, pop and soul to Christmas pantomime and questionable cabaret. I had been on television twice and played on the radio countless times. Joining a band was a new prospect though, and when that fateful day finally came, I drove into London to meet my future band mates, the whole time feeling like something very special was about to happen.

I connected with my new colleagues instantly. Maz, the lead singer, was born in London to Brazilian diplomats, and I got the sense life had been good to her growing up in Belgravia. Maz had this glacial slow calm talking voice, compared to her dynamically volcanic singing voice which was quite something.

At some point I commented, "Maz, you could put any anxious mind at ease. You could voice audiobooks or something."

She told me to "fuck off mate. I'm supposed to sing not speak."

I liked that line. Maz was the most superb lead singer and oozed the number-one-most-important-front-person asset. You couldn't take your eyes off her. I'll never forget our first chat discussing the finer points of Minnie Ripperton. As we spoke, I noticed she had a kids dinosaur toy weaved into her hair. I loved that. I knew that this lady was going to be full of surprises, her 'never a dull moment' spirit would be the theme of our band's relationship.

Vic, our third musketeer, was the guitar player and a sort of ying to Maz's yang. They had a Lennon McCartney style thing going on, something akin to a Keith Richards and Mick Jagger or Karen O and Nick Zinner. Vic was born in Sweden to British obsessed parents who moved to London when he was one. When I first met Vic, he was topless, had a cigarette in his mouth and was reading *Catcher in the Rye* whilst simultaneously changing guitar strings. Clearly a multitasker I thought.

Vic had effortlessly sleek, shiny, envy-inciting raven black hair. Curiously he always had it cut in a way that looked like a bowl had been placed on his head. I would later learn Vic always cut his own hair, his bangs precisely covering just enough of his eyes so he could hide if he had to, a look only really suitable for a guitarist. In other professions involving eye contact it's not an ideal style. Vic was shy as can be, his floppy fringe was his comfort blanket. We all need one of those I reckon, even up and coming rock and roll guitarists.

We were just scratching the surface of our musical and professional friendships, but it was clear I was in good company.

The Soho's were born that day underneath the west London railway arch and in my mind that's the exact moment ME turned to WE.

With my drumsticks in hand, I had tapped my way so far.

I had been incessant, like water dripping through a cracked gutter in a rainstorm.

Tap, tap, tap.

Let's see where it will take me. Or should I say, let's see where it will take WE!

Tap, tap, tap.

The year – 1997

Location – Oxford

Subject – The Soho's

It's still tap tap, tap, only it's in quick succession, like continuous fire-crackers being set off above me. It's absolutely raining cats and dogs outside. The heavy droplets hitting the roof of the van, affectionately named 'Rosie', is quite a sound, oddly soothing, like staring at a camp-fire.

With time passing my fledging band had taken flight. The scene is now the picturesque English town of Oxford, home of the world-famous university, punting, and Radiohead. We're not a massive band yet, we can't even fill the second smallest room at this dingy but very friendly music venue. I remember the posters for all the upcoming shows lining the walls of the dressing room, all bands we knew personally, most of them say sold out, all of them boldly stating they are playing the considerably larger main room next door. This bothered me to such an extent that I just hung out in the van all day writing Pop positive affirm-ations into my diary whilst listening to the English weather batter 'Rosie.' I was stewing in jealousy. I knew I would put this negative energy to good use later that night – I always did. The songs were going to have an angsty slant to their swing that evening. Back then my ambitious nature made me very competitive. I believe this is a good habit a young band should have, but my eyes have always been bigger than my belly, and when it came to *the band*, my appetite was especially ferocious.

I wanted to have it all.

(Diary extract)

I want to be like Coca Cola.
WORLD-WIDE FAMOUS.

Oxford was just another day on a three-month tour of playing rooms filled with next to no one, a realisation that day which had really pushed me and my usual titanium-lined confidence to its limits. I was impatient, sure, but deep down I knew success has to be earned. It's the 'off days' when you're trying the absolute hardest to push your boulder up the hills which are sent to test you.

I was still reassured, knowing that we were doing what all the best bands do. We were paying dues by honing our craft, going from town to town, playing songs with every ounce our hearts and souls could possibly muster, playing to anyone who cared to watch or listen. What happened on stage is what fed my underlying faith. We were a force to be reckoned with: we were a three-piece band – in my opinion, the classic, most bestest line-up combination there can be. Think Cream, The Police, Nirvana, Jimi Hendrix, Green Day! I love the musical and physical space you gain from being in a three-piece. Even the symmetry of the band appeals to me, as a three piece the formation on stage is best described as pyramidesque. As we played, I always imagined our band's full energy being funneled through our collective trifecta of pyramidic positioning, throwing our vibes into the room with force!

Well, that night Maz changed things up. She felt, due to the lack of attendees, she would do her gig in front of the stage where said attendees should have been. Now myself and Vic of course didn't have a problem with that. "Whatever is the vibe is the vibe", Vic said during an exhale of one of his signature menthol cigarettes. In between and during singing duties Maz cartwheeled her way around that darkened concert hall like a rockstar ballerina.

After the show we shared a moment, we talked about the gig.

"I just needed the leg room, darling," she said whilst eating a crisp from a bag of Walkers salt and vinegar, sitting on one of our well-travelled flight cases as elegantly as a high society woman sitting in a Parisian patisserie eating a freshly baked croissant.

Regardless of the audience sizes, we were simply undeniable, and in my opinion when you're 'simply undeniable', it's only a matter of time until success makes its welcome appearance. Until then we would go from city to city, from country to country, like a gang of musical pirates following our invisible and fully improvised internal maps of best laid plans and imperishable ambitions. We were completely rigorous and unrelenting in our pursuit.

That night in Oxford we played to thirty people and a dog.

I even knew the dog's name: Draculvalius aka Drac. He was Chalky the venue owner's dog.

Chalky was the lead singer of an almost famous goth punk band from the 80s called 'Deth Hook'. We liked Chalky. We played his venue a lot. He was good to us when he didn't need to be. Regardless of the small number of eyes and ears present, we still played like it was a packed stadium and, with all my youthful confidence, I took great solace in knowing it would be the best show this audience saw all year. There was actually twenty more people than last time. It was progress!

After loading up our gear at the end of the night, I relaxed by lying down in the back of Rosie the van. A handful of newly acquired fans from the evening's show had joined us to drink what was left of the warm Red Stripe beer laid on by Chalky and Drac. I had a puff of a joint being passed round, then watched the stars through a sliver of window. The stars were so bright. If I squinted, I am sure I could even see Jym.

It was possibly the effects of the grass, but watching the stars shimmering in the pitch-black sky gave me a rare moment of reflection. I remember the distinct feeling of happiness; I was happy about the band's musical endeavours. Yeah sure, no one knew us yet, but to me that just felt more like a technicality. Just like Grandma and Grandpa I had found my true calling, and just like them I was following it to the hilt.

As Rosie rolled off, there was laughing and singing, lots of joyful vibrations: a very good scene. I continued to enjoy these vibes as the bus made its way to the budget hotel situated on the outskirts of Oxford. The types of hotels we stayed at were never in the city. They were hidden away out of sight, often by a motorway, almost always next to a petrol station. The budget dictated our choice of accommodation. "Cheap and cheerful," Eddie our tour manager slash bus driver slash roadie would call them. I don't know about cheerful, but they were certainly cheap. If we couldn't afford a hotel, we would all sleep in Rosie, or crash on generous fans' floors or sofas. When we could afford a hotel, we would get two rooms. I bunked with our multi-tasking tour manager. This would be deemed 'the quiet room'; my musical compadres' room would be considered 'the party room.' The typical party room always featured these necessities for an excellent time: a boom box, whatever alcohol was left lying around, a shower cap for the fire alarm and a wet towel for the little gap under the door to stop both cigarette and weed wafting through the establishment. Oh, and I mustn't forget – an Allen key for the inevitable locked window. You have to go up a star or two in hotel accommodation to have a freely opening window. A party room should always be positioned the furthest possible distance from the 'quiet room', ideally at the end of a corridor.

The 'quiet room' was my sanctuary and I believe I'd mastered the art of sharing early on in our touring adventures. I got into the habit of creating a little room within the room, and this would be done by laying the mattress on the floor and then turning the bed frame on its side, then I used the spare blanket from the wardrobe to drape over the upturned bed frame creating my very own tent-like space. I felt far more comfortable in my little rock and roll wigwam, and I eventually called this type of Feng Shui tenacity, *'creating my own vibe'*. You always find little tricks to make yourself more comfortable on the road and this was one of mine. My early touring eccentricities didn't end there though. For example, in a bid to remain creative on days off, I'd got into the habit of drawing on the bedroom wall behind the hotel's obligatory mass-produced dreary decorative painting. There's always one, sometimes two, often a trio of stones or a local bridge, perhaps a man or a woman holding an umbrella. Perhaps you are familiar with these artistic treats?

I saw an exciting Banksy-esque opportunity and ran with it. I took whatever picture off the wall and sketched, preferably with a felt tip, sometimes with paints, crayons, or just the branded hotel pencil that sits on the desk. My wall art was mostly abstract: no drawings of ponies, flowers, or drum kits.

When it comes to my behind-the-painting-painting series, I am sure by now all of my artistic works have been discovered and painted over, but if you ever find yourself staying in a one-, two- or three-star hotel anywhere in the world have a look behind your rooms artwork to see if you find any of my old masterpieces. I believe there was a particularly great example behind a large photograph of a boat in a Super 8 Motel in Cincinnati, it's the one on the freeway next to the gas station heading North into the city.

"Fair fucks to ya!" Eddie first said when he saw my works.

He did say fair fucks a lot but not as much as his second and third favourite complimentary terms – 'Boss' and 'Beltin' – two expressions which only truly come to life with Eddie's very own thick Liverpudlian accent.

"OH, THAT'S BELTIN THAT IS LAD"

Or

"THAT'S PROPER BOSS THAT IS KIDDA"

Banksy-inspired art aside, it was actually a move made by our industrious Eddie that inspired the rather vandalistic art project, a 'move' so cunningly good it must be shared. It was a year prior that we arrived in America to do a showcase with a bunch of other acts for a big record label we would eventually sign to – a couple of pop stars, a hip hop group, and us. We landed in Texas and promptly went about checking our rental gear in preparation for the performance the next day. This is important as there's absolutely always something missing, like it's somehow mystically written into every rental company's job description. It's always roulette as to which instrument would be affected and on this trip it was my turn to draw the short straw in the form of a missing drum carpet.

The drum carpet is vital for me as I tend to play with such ferocious energy that the carpet helps hold everything in place, and without it my cymbals slide one way, my bass drum the other. It's comical to watch but not funny for me. Without a drum rug in the early days, whilst playing squat parties or in people's houses, I often had to tie my drum stands to a radiator or anything fixed on the wall behind me. You gotta do what ya gotta do, right?

I once heard The Who's Keith Moon would nail his gear to the stage with a hammer. I must admit I haven't needed to try that one yet, if anyone was to do that of course it would be 'Mooney,' wouldn't it? Keith's lion-like ferocity behind those drums was undeniably iconic.

To the rug-less dilemma at hand: "Not a problem dear boy! Needs must!" Eddie eagerly exclaimed.

There were never problems with Eddie, only solutions. He was very much 'a can do' kinda guy. He taught me a lot about the power of DIY. Eddie had DIY DNA, that's why we called him Swiss Army Eddie.

Eddie's plan to solve the missing rug problem was to go back to the hotel next to the motorway and cut the carpet around his bed with a sharp blade. He sliced as tightly as he could against the frame so it would be completely unnoticeable to the untrained eye. Once finished he asked me to lift up the end of the bed, and as I did, he pulled my new drum carpet free. When the bed was back in position it looked exactly as it did when we first arrived.

Villainous Genius!

We had to do this trick more than once.

With hindsight I would like to suggest it was probably our very own version of trashing hotel rooms, but with artistic intentions.

Never has a nickname been more suitable than 'Swiss Army Eddie.' The man knew all the places to get things done on a shoestring budget like ours. What wasn't budget was his experience and sense of humour. This was priceless. The man knew every single breakfast deal at every local cafe and restaurant within a thirty-mile radius of his current position. This was pre-Google Maps; it was an extraordinary ability. It was like he had an inbuilt sonar radar for cheese on toast. A 'deal' would be classed as anything under three quid, ideal for our meagre funds. Eddie's absolute favourite food was cheese followed by potatoes, and he always liked to start every meal with dessert. "It all ends up in the same place" was his logic.

We'd been a band for three years, and we'd been on the road more than we'd been off it. What I was finding out in real time was that life on tour really was my kind of life. I hated being home and loved travelling with my friends, on the way to play music in a new city. It felt like freedom: play where you want, paint where you want, and answer to nothing but the music.

Our very first album hadn't even come out yet.

It was still salad days for the group, good vibes, and high fives all the way. We had one job: we were there to put on a show and put on a show we did. I was constantly hearing how incredible we were after each performance. I mean they couldn't all be lying, could they? We were using our fine-tuned musicality and telekinetic rhythmic synergy to keep everyone on their toes, ourselves included.

Back to Oxford. It was the start of a run of eight consecutive shows. This was a lot, but we didn't know any better. We loved to play. At the time eight gigs in a row was fairly standard for us. Our record tally of shows on the bounce was fourteen. I now call that back-to-back bananas! What was different about this run was that on the final gig we would be supporting a big-time soul singer Valerie Red at the Astoria, a now demolished 3,000 capacity venue on London's Charing Cross Road. All the shows flew by in the way touring always does – all but the eighth show that is. There were two reasons for this. The first was that we were uncharacteristically awful, yeah yeah yeah, I know, but even after all my own hype our group wasn't exempt from the occasional 'off night.' Time on stage moves so slowly when you suck. What's perhaps more frustrating is that when it's going great it goes by like a flash of lightning.

I wish all the good shows lasted forever and all the bad ones were gone in a blink of an eye.

"Oh, my days, that was butters," Maz our lead singer exclaimed when we finally headed off stage. Our guitarist Vic simply called it: "Murders." Even after a few years I was still getting used to my band mates' thoroughbred London lingo. Translation: BAD!

No performer can expect to dodge the inevitable "off show" curse. They happen to everyone from time to time. It's just part of being a touring band; it's really no biggie.

It's always best to accept they happen and move on quickly. Next! I left the stage to visit the upstairs dressing rooms in need of a fresh shirt and a drink. On my way I passed Valerie Red, the beautiful soul-drenched rebel rockstar whose night it really was. Her name emblazoned in the impossible-to-miss bright show biz lights above the entrance of the theatre made it clear we were very thankful, very temporary guests in her world.

"Which one are you then?" she asked in her instantly recognisable North London tones.

"I'm the drummer. Thank you so much for letting us play."

She didn't say anything, only paused to light a cigarette and with a subtle glance our eyes met before she wandered off in a puff of Marlboro smoke, cool A F.

With an extra spring in my step, I continued with my task. Donning a fresh shirt and cradling four bottles of room temperature beer, I proceeded to join the rest of 'the gang' to pack away our gear. We were about to have four days off. At the time I didn't particularly enjoy days off, especially days off at home. Fortunately for me, as I was wondering what to do with this down-time predicament, one of those extra springy steps helped conjure a most ambitious idea.

The sublimely planted seed of the idea I believe was dropped that morning when I discovered my Irish troubadour friend Waldo would be playing in New York City on Halloween in two days' time. I happened to know this because every morning I'd check the band's website to update it on all our comings and goings. Whilst doing this I always took a moment to check out what any of our musical friends were up to. That morning, I happened to visit my Irish buddy's website whilst using the hotel's complimentary business centre computer, which was basically a computer-sized desk hidden behind a few large pot plants and a coffee machine in the weathered reception area. Yeah, in 1997 the smartphones weren't a thing yet, that supposed luxury wouldn't be hitting our shelves for another nine years.

It didn't occur to me then that this was the solution to my 'time off' dilemma, but while I lugged guitar speakers and drum cases onto the narrow-cobbled alley behind the venue in anticipation of Rosie's imminent arrival, I really couldn't imagine a better way to spend my upcoming time off. I mean why not eh? Nip off to the Big Apple and play music with my folksy friend. Get in.

It seemed a plan had formulated. Was it achievable though?

I told Cynthia of my idea as we finished loading Rosie. She was always supportive of any bandmember's outside endeavours.

She said, "You guys are making a movie, the more you push and try different things the better your movie will be."

She was a great manager, always full of wisdom and philosophy, something she attributed to a tough childhood and living her pre-music business life as a quick-on-her-feet super successful New York Attorney of law.

I was off!

On the way to the tube station to catch an easy ride home, I called Waldo to tell him my plans. I could already hear by the funky ring tone that he was stateside. When he picked up without even saying hello, I told him I was coming over.

"Yes, Pop," he happily shouted back in response.

"Text me the info. I will see you there my friend." Click!

Just like that I hung up: straight to the point, no messing. Precious phone credit intact.

As I sat on the rickety old Northern line heading home to Belsize Park, I wrote something in my diary that Grandpa once said to me. His words, as they often did, had been flying through my head.

"DREAMS ARE LIKE ORANGES!"

Grandpa elaborated on this citric smile with the most excellent insight I am about to share with you.

(Diary extract)

Dreaming is the moment you begin processing all of what you've seen, read, heard, and most importantly felt in your day-to-day life.

For you to be able to absorb and process the worst, best, most important parts of your daily life you need to dream.

Just like getting to the good part of an orange, the dreaming that goes on in your mind when you slumber is like the peeling back of your most mundane, standard, abstract, obscure, happy, sad, sometimes nonsensical, dreaded or even horrifying thoughts.

This can lead to some serious brain gymnastics.

To use another comparison, which Grandpa was very fond of doing, he said the equivalent was food being digested in your tummy turning into energy. Dreams and what you dream is basically your brain digesting its visual and emotional dinner.

"It's just like the peeling of an orange to get to the juicy delicious part."

I always love jotting down these wordy memories and this evening was no different; that is, until my writing came to an abrupt halt when a boatload of boisterous pissed-up football fans boarded the train, their rowdy energy spoiling my train of thought. I decided to get off at the next stop, a minor inconvenience really as the cab home was six quid and six quid for a good vibe is priceless.

When I got in, I left my bag at the front door in anticipation of our next journey together. I then immediately hit up the loaf of bread which in our house was traditionally kept in the fridge. I stuck two slices into the chrome toaster and took a moment to catch up with Elvin who lived next door but was currently crashing on the sofa because his missus kicked him out.

The toast popped which thankfully saved me from getting too deep into Elvin's bizarre chat – something about his favourite TV show about aliens.

"Ya know they're already here Pop. They're here I tell ya!" he rambled as I left the room, only to return to the kitchen to liberally apply salty Irish butter to my hot toasty bread.

I ask you this, is there anything better than hot buttery toast?

The simplicity is outstanding.

I've got to say breakfast foods in general are just the most ideal meal when you get home late – scrambled eggs, toast, cereal, pancakes – they always hit the spot just right, but especially during the witching hours.

Grandpa and Grandma would say, "breakfast always spoils your lunch." I somewhat agree, but to limit such a cornucopia of tasty treats to morning time never made sense to me.

That night two slices of buttery toast were just not enough to satisfy, so I went all in for a round two only this time I doubled up, two for me and two for Benjy who owned the house and lived on the third floor.

Benjy was minted. He was one of those trust fund kids and never had to worry about a thing. Such a lovely guy, but there was definitely a real heavy sadness about him. I think it came from not having enough love when he was a kid. That, and the realisation as he got older that having everything so young zaps your desire to do anything when you grow up.

We met through Benjy's weed dealer, Sunny, who lived in the house with Benjy. The relationship worked great until Sunny ended up selling so much weed in the area that he had enough to buy his own house out of town. It was a tag team scenario: the day Sunny moved out I moved in. Benjy always wanted to play drums so, like Sunny, I provided a service beyond tenancy – that's a real rich person trait.

I heard a few years ago that Benjy gave away everything he owned and became one of those people who paint themselves silver and stand completely still in Covent Garden. I can believe it, to be honest.

"Salutations Pop, what can I do you for?" Benjy's baritone voice announced on my arrival.

A deal was quickly struck, and I borrowed Benjy's computer as a fair trade for the buttery hot toast. I planned to book my plane tickets on one of those websites that finds you the cheapest, last-minute deals. Yeah, even back then that was a thing! Mere seconds after typing into the web browser, I was onto a winner and two hundred pounds later, I was all set. NYC here I come.

With my travel arrangements complete I headed down to my bedroom in the basement. My modest setup included a drum kit, a mattress on the floor and an enormous furry tiger print bean bag. I also had a wardrobe built into the slightly faded pale, pink-coloured walls which homed my ever-increasing 70s inspired wardrobe. The room was spartan which suited me just fine.

I played drums for a bit and then set aside the clothes that I would be wearing for my early morning wake up and subsequent New York adventure. I planned to sleep in my own bed, instead I fell asleep like a baby on my marshmallow mushroom cloud bean bag oblivious to the fact I would be waking up only a few hours later. Who needs sleep when you're living your best life?

Plane journeys are for snoozing anyway. There's nothing better you can do with the time. Watch a film on a screen the size of a match box? No, thank, you! Back then I was already a seasoned traveller and had my long-haul air travel routine mapped out precisely.

It began with me consuming two Frankie Vallis (Valium) on immediate arrival at my seat – taking them any earlier can often result in unforeseen circumstances like falling asleep in the departure lounge before your flight is called. Yes, I speak from experience. Before drifting off I asked the steward / stewardess to wake me when they began serving food. I am not one for missing a meal even if it is plane food. I am also not afraid to ring the bell in preparation for doing my best Oliver Twist impression. "Please sir / mam, can I have some more…?"

Out of necessity I also adopted the imperative flying trick of buying a sandwich before I jump on any flight. This sandwich was a *break in case of emergency* type scenario sammie, a convenient solution if you get extra hungry and a good way to avoid the *hangers*, a curse I suffer immensely from.

My favourite 'go to' sandwich was the simple yet classic cheese sandwich. With my cheese sammie I liked slices of cheddar but preferred it grated. I always enjoyed white bread more than brown, but with a baguette I was in sandwich heaven. If I got both grated cheese and a freshly baked baguette, I was having an extra champion day.

For this trip I'd been lucky to book the last window seat available. I enjoy gazing out of the window while eating an airplane supper. The food can be hit or miss, but I really don't care. I love the experience of sky dining. After a mid-flight bite, I would almost always without fail fall right back to sleep and a few hours later wake up ready to go.

That was my plan which I still use on flights to this day – minus the Frankie's as they have been replaced with the rather less addictive CBD gummy bears which I think work just as marvellously, if not better!

The Year – 1997 (February)

Location – British Airways Boeing 747, seat 32 d

Destination – Newark International Airport, USA

Time – Early Afternoon, Eastern Standard Time

Emotion – Discombobulated

I woke up, hovering somewhere over New York with a flight attendant gently tapping my arm. I can only imagine that she'd been calling my name for quite some time as my sleeping mind slowly began to register her Irish accent. I instantly felt the frustration in her voice.

"Wake up, Mr Morrison. MR MORRISON, WAKE UP."

I pulled down my black wayfarer shades to look at her and apologised for my tardiness. Her stony face told me that she'd lost her patience somewhere over the Atlantic.

"Time to straighten your seat and pull up your window blind Mr Morrison, we are going to land shortly."

"Sure thing."

The Valium knocked me out cold.

My plan had gone out the window. It appeared I had slept the whole way.

I imagine they tried to wake me for dinner, but the combination of tiredness and sedative made it an impossible task.

This was a splendid example of where my *break in case of an emergency* cheese sandwich comes in. I was most fortunate in the Heathrow airport sandwich sweep stakes because as I cracked open my grated cheese on near enough fresh baguette. I already knew it is going to be a champion day.

I devoured the sandwich and finished up with a few sips of a very meek half tepid off brand cola. I brushed the crumbs off my lap and threw a fresh piece of minty chewing gum into my mouth, and only then did I draw up the blind to look at the huge mass of land below me.

The state of New York is vast and green, the surrounding areas of the Big Apple aka Manhattan, are by no means all skyscraper and concrete. It's not too dissimilar to the rolling hills of green parts of Britain, that is with one really big exception.

BEARS!

New York State has bears – lots and lots of bears.

As I looked at the land below zipping past, I thought about its immense beauty and its equally immense and not-to-be-messed with grizzlies. I thought about this nature-inspired insecurity whilst tapping a samba beat on my legs. I obviously got really into it as I didn't even notice the plane landing. Samba can do that to you. As I disembarked the paraffin budgie, I felt super energised and every bit ready for my first day of New York adventuring.

My first impression of Newark International Airport is best described as 'heaving'. Not a problem. I was already well versed in this hustle. I navigated myself through the travelling throngs and cleared US customs without a hitch. I then made my way through to baggage claim to begin the usual tedious waiting around for bags to start appearing.

In London I had every intention of carrying my small bag onto the airplane as hand luggage, after all, this is what I usually do. I don't know what happened though for something came over me whilst checking in at Heathrow. Perhaps it was the early morning mind-fog, but at the very last moment I changed tack and me and my bag parted ways. I regretted this decision immensely as the 25th minute passed, and I watched every bag but mine emerge from the conveyor belt.

I knew this type of thing happened and with all the flying I did, I knew it was bound to happen to me eventually. I saw it as the touring musician's rite of passage, an accomplishment of sorts, a badge of honour.

I waited five more minutes and when the conveyor belt finally came to a halt, I shrugged it off, and took it as my cue to leave. I didn't feel the need to make a complaint or cause fuss. It was an open-and-shut case: my bag was gone, and I was eager keep moving.

That day my plan was to get one of New York's iconic taxi cabs into the big city. I made sure I was heading in the right direction for the golden yellow chariots by asking a gang of youthful Jet Blue air stewards and stewardesses.

"Excuse me, which way to the famous yellow taxi cabs?"

I got giggly smiles followed by a series of hands pointing me on my way. In fact, the signs were clearly marked, and I knew exactly where I was going. Here's the thing, I rather enjoy talking to people, even if it's just asking questions – mundane or vibrational. I think talking is your friend and I certainly like to chew the fat, it's one of my hobbies, although I am not totally sure you can really class talking as a hobby.

I carried on walking through the buzzing airport until I reached the exit and my presence signalled the huge automatic doors to open, and as they did I was instantly greeted with a whole new sensory experience. The mixture of exhaust fumes, humidity and the very distinct aroma of…

AMERICA

Now if you asked me to describe the smell of the United States, I would say you're in luck because after much thought on this subject I have a rather ambiguous, but very descriptive answer.

WATER!

It's identical to the taste of water.

But water has no taste you say?

This is true, but you know when it's water and you know when it's not right? It's unmistakable.

You can feel America like that. It's in the air and just like water it's too big a presence on planet earth to ignore or avoid. Well, at least that's how I felt about the place.

To me, being in America back then always conjured memories of movies, bands, and lots of other things I always thought were absolutely terrific.

I mean what about Mrs Nancy Johnson's fabulous invention, the hand-cranked ice cream machine. ICE CREAM I tell ya, all created right here in the old U....S....of....A!

The ideal place for a Wonderboy like me.

I walked through the electric doors and despite my lost luggage I felt very lucky indeed. This luck was promptly emphasised by a very good sight – no queue for the cabs. Queuing for taxi cabs at airports is very dull. Queues in general are lousy, but there's something a little extra about waiting in lines at airports. Just when you think you're free they get you with one last sneaky queue, literally one for the road. From my point of view though airport related queuing definitely should be looked upon like some weird form of interpretive art.

I could see my ride up ahead, and as I made my way to the patiently waiting vehicle I passed by at least twenty restless cabbies waiting for their next me. I thought about these folks and what they do whilst waiting in limbo for their next gig. I was most pleased to see a group of them playing chess on the trunk of one of their cars. Chess is a splendid board game based completely on wits and strategy. My Dad taught me as a child, and I still play today.

I now believe releasing albums on major labels requires the same type of cunning skills.

As I walked past I asked, "Who's winning lads?"

They just stared at me blankly, fazed and confused.

I smiled nonetheless.

Whilst on the subject of New York cabs, I was recently told that since the 1980s almost all New York taxi cabs are ex-police cars. It may or may not be true, but I am partial to collecting fun facts.

I opened the back door and immediately noticed the back seat was covered in cigarettes burn marks. The old ciggy burn always reminds me of music venue dressing rooms, European motorway service station bathrooms and forever this particular journey.

As I clambered into the back of the car, I thought about the old saying, "Oh, to be a fly on the wall".

I then switched that phrase up and wondered, "What if each cigarette burn could tell a story?" That's especially interesting with the New York City cop car connection.

You could have had a bank robber sitting in the same seat as one of the guys from The Ramones.

Cool!

As I settled into the back of the classic yellow travel machine the immediate difference between my beloved London black cab was clear. For one, they are tiny. For such a widely documented nation of large individuals they seem to have the smallest taxi cabs. Perhaps they have the smallest bank robbers too? Mini cabs indeed!

After getting in, I turned to the driver.

"The Gershwin hotel please, mate."

I said this already knowing exactly how my British accent was going to land. This wasn't my first rodeo!

Coming to America became a regular occurrence once we signed our record deal. This was before the world got a whole lot smaller with smartphones and social media. Back then it was impossible for me not to notice that being an Englishman in America had a delicious hint of mystery about it, a novelty almost.

During these early visits I couldn't help noticing a few words that seemed to highlight the English accent most endearingly. For example, starting a conversation with "excuse me" in an English accent instantly made you sound like a cast member for one of those made-for-TV period dramas. Let's not forget the modern but highly effective '*mate*' which always seemed to do something rather mystical to across the pond conversations.

In this situation the word *mate* utilised all the cheekiest aspects of my English tones, specifically the London accent, the posh cockney, aka the poshney. I hereby declare for the record that I am guilty of a little poshney from time to time.

I watched the taxi driver's face as my words landed with great effect. His eyes, which were once focused on something of interest way off in the distance, immediately shifted to me.

"A Brit!" The surprised sounding cabbie responded in his thick New York accent, the reaction akin to seeing a mermaid, shooting star or something equally brilliant.

"How ya doin'? How's the Queen? Tell her she owes me ten bucks," he said cracking himself up.

"Mate, that's quite some laugh you have there."

He goes on to tell me that his ex-wife would say it reminded her of a lawn mower running out of gas. A further giggle was had. Laughing to me is just like having a good conversation – another great friend.

"I'm Pauly," he introduced himself.

Pauly was a portly chap with thick blackish, greyish slicked back hair. He was smiling an excellent smile. I could see his gold front tooth, a very powerful look in anyone. I liked him instantly.

Behind Pauly's smiley face hanging underneath the rear-view mirror from a rosary bead necklace was his NYC taxi driver license. I couldn't help but notice his second name. DiMaggio. Absolutely brilliant! Couldn't be more New York Italian if you tried.

"What's your name English?" Pauly asked in his classic New York tones.

"I'm Pop Morrison. Pleased to meet you Pauly DiMaggio."

Pauly stopped mid-way fastening his seatbelt to look inquisitively at me in the rear-view mirror until he remembered what was hanging below it. I watched as the cogs in his mind turned while he put two and two together, when four appeared he smiled his excellent gold tooth smile and I clocked for the first time in our journey that he had eyes like a robber's dog, kind eyes, but eyes like a robber's dog.

"Come on then Sherlock, off to the Gershwin, I won't spare the horses," Pauly said with an attempt at an aristocratic English twang.

"I can tell I'm in good company," I say mid laugh.

As my yellow chariot began to roll, we started our journey by joining Newark airport's never-ending one-way maze of road works. When we finally hit the highway, I could see the most fabulous sight way off in the distance. The marvellous view grew steadily closer with every mile that passed – the great island of Manhattan. With that iconic sight on my horizon Pauly D and I began a rather memorable conversation.

"English, did you know New York was originally called New Amsterdam?" asked Pauly. Wonderstuff!

Pauly's a film buff and at every other street corner he would have a cinematic fact to tell me. He talked animatedly about a 70s movie called *The Warriors* as we whizzed past a park that featured in the cult classic. He said it was one of his favourite films ever. I said I know it and that I recognised the green expanse, but I really didn't – inconsequential I think because now I do, and to this day every time I pass 'Riverside Park' that lovely green space by the Hudson River, I'm reminded of that film I've still not seen. And right behind that memory?

The most New York man I've ever met, Mr Pauly DiMaggio.

As we weaved through Manhattan, I instantly felt the endless possibility New York City had to further fuel my enthusiasm for life. I've always loved the big apple, the city is a melting pot of tastes, sounds, colours and smells. I had the window wound all the way down in a bid to soak in every last drop of the *VIBE*.

There's always lots of time to take in these *vibes* from the back of a cab, not least the madness of NYC traffic. The amount of cars versus road space is grossly out of proportion. New York was built for a horse and carriage, not for Mr Ford or Miss Mercedes. Space is at a premium on the well-worn roads. I have always been cool with it, but then again I've never lived here. I was taking it all in like any Wonderboy should.

One moment the smell of warm, sweet, sugar-coated almonds washed through the cab, a block later you got the permanent NYC fixture – the all-American hot dog stand and their steaming hot Franks filling the air with a subtle offending pong dispersed only by the smell of thousands of hot engines attempting to roam the roads.

The New York street hot dog bothered me. I was not a fan. I must say it's rare that you'll find a food that I don't like but the New York street dog is just that. It turns my tummy. I have to think it's the atmosphere eating curbside that adds something significant to this supposed New York street delicacy?

Moving on to…

Manhattan, Manhattan.

I was mid-town. It was mid-afternoon and the city was buzzing with activity. From the back of Pauly's cab I remember zoning in on all the entrepreneurial street market hustlers peddling their cheap counterfeit sunglasses, handbags and New York inspired souvenirs right there on the polka dot bubble gum-stained sidewalks. We passed hordes of them. And not only that they were all choc-a-bloc busy with business.

"Fair play", I said out loud as we made our way into Chinatown with its permanent neon lit window displays, the sensory message beckoning you and your taste buds with supremely bright lights and hot tasty food. New York's Chinatown is a wondrous place for taste, but notoriously bad for smells. On a hot day like this, it can go either way. Pauly said it best:

"Some days this place smells like the inside of the New York Nicks locker room after a good old ass whooping."

He'd been cracking jokes and suppling one-liners like this since the moment I got in the car. It was obvious he had a gift. I told him how I could imagine him being a whip-smart stand-up comedian, but he waved this off, gingerly claiming that he was too old. I told him you're never too old to follow your dreams.

"Fortune favours the bold, brother," I concluded.

He responded with a 'dad joke.' His only clanger of our journey.

"Hey Pop, who's cauliflower's brother?"

"I don't know Pauly who is cauliflower's brother?"

"Broccoli, B R O c c o l i... It's a stinker, ain't it?"

Pauly asked this knowing full well he knew the answer already. I looked out the window and silently agreed with him.

Talk about stinker, that day in New York it turned out that either the wind was blowing in the opposite direction, or the bins had recently been collected as all I could smell through my defiantly open window was delicious Chinese food.

The whole thing left me with a ravenous thirst. Altitude and Valium can do that to you. It was time to make a quick bodega pit stop where I purchased a bottle of needlessly expensive arctic chilled water in a fancy glass bottle and twenty-five scratch cards. The water instantly gave me brain freeze to which I blindly cursed out loud. Once the painful chill subsided, I took a particularly shiny pound coin from my pocket and began to scratch away. At some point Pauly clocked what I was doing and asked very sincerely in advance to borrow some money if I win.

"Hey English, front me some clams if you win, will ya?"

As we pulled up to the Gershwin Hotel I responded with equal sincerity.

"Sure thing, Pauly.'

During my formative years, The Gershwin Hotel on the east side of 27th street was my favourite place to stay in the city of Manhattan. I don't know what it was about the place, but 'I' and 'IT' just clicked. A mere stone's throw away from the epic art deco Empire State Building, its central location right in the thick of it, provided you with the full no holds barred New York experience.

What more could you ask for?

It certainly fully catered for all my needs. Hey, I appreciate you are possibly thinking that this hotel doesn't sound *cheap and cheerful!* It doesn't sound like one of those aforementioned hidden motorway establishments. Well, it certainly wasn't.

It was a bold act of suavity that meant this four-starrer was my NYC home from home. You see, it just so happened that our previously agreed record deal was a pretty sweet situation for us. It was a unique deal because it was for North America only, meaning we could do what we wanted for the rest of the world. Cynthia's inspired idea was to sign separate record deals for each country. Something which would turn out to be a super smart, ahead-of-its-time move that would later serve us very well indeed, its pertaining perk would be that upon signing our fat record deal advance would be in dollars, not pounds. Cynthia set us each up with American bank accounts and had our share wired across. It was more zeros than I'd ever seen before, but more importantly, my bank card had pictures of puppies on it, and better yet apparently every time I used it a little bit of money went towards helping dogs.

We each kept our money in America with the intention of spending it solely in America, like if we signed a deal in Australia, we would keep our money there and only use it when we were down under.

It made sense to me, and Cynthia's plan was coming to life with America being the first to come and play ball. What it really meant though was every time we crossed the pond, we were what you would call *BALLING*.

This was just a juicy cherry on top of why we loved going stateside. Our American appreciation was based more on the fact it felt like stuff was happening for us over there. It felt like we were getting some of the respect we deserved, whereas in our home country, the not-so-Great Britain, we just couldn't seem to turn our spark into fire.

I was grateful for this minute taste of success. I think it kept us all motivated. We collectively took the glimpse as a little green confirmation tick that our musical instincts were correct, a tip of the hat, as if to say, *KEEP IT UP. DON'T GIVE UP.*

So upon arrival to the Gershwin Hotel, I was greeted warmly at the noble brownstone building.

"Travelling light, Mr Pop?" Howard the hotel concierge asked.

"They lost my bag buddy. I believe they were sick of carrying such an elaborate wardrobe."

Howard was unsure whether to laugh or not, so I gladly led the way, and a few jovial moments later he eagerly led me into the hotel's comforting lavender scented reception area.

"Have a great stay, Mr Pop."

"Cheers mate."

The hotel's name, after the legendary composer George Gershwin, already gave the place a homely feel for any inspired musician. The hotel also seemed to have an ethos aimed at being more 'sympathetic to the artistic clientele'.

It's a ridiculous phrase I know, and one I have heard a lot in my time.

I always interpreted it to mean the establishment was more relaxed on the rules. They don't go ballistic if you smoked in the rooms or played loud music at night. Perhaps you'd find yourself riding a bicycle down the hallways while loudly reciting Talking Heads lyrics in just your underwear and a bandana: something like that wouldn't be a problem, for example.

Artistically sympathetic indeed.

Every time I stayed at the Gershwin, I would always get Room 612 or 613 directly opposite. Don't ask me why. Out of the two rooms, 612 was my favourite as the windows overlooked the buzz of central Manhattan, whereas 613 looked out to a car park and the place where all the restaurants on the block kept their rubbish, or should I say 'trash'. If I ever got 613 the curtains remained closed for the duration of my stay. There's not one part of that view I wish to see.

I was very casual about my lost luggage, wasn't I?

I didn't really care you see. That's why I left the airport without even reporting my loss, in fact I would go as far as saying it didn't even register as one, besides, I already knew exactly where I needed to go to replenish my lost items.

The place was called, The Treasure Closet: a sort of holy destination for a kid like me in a band. Being in the scene, I'd heard about the Treasure Closet many times. *If you're ever in NYC you gotta go* would be a guaranteed recommendation from any fellow musician from the Big Apple. The store's word of mouth was mighty.

I recall 'mighty' meant nothing to me at the time though, as the only mighty feeling I had was hunger. I was mighty hungry!

First things first. FOOD!

Not long after my freshen up I was back out on the busy streets of Manhattan when I decided a quick three dollar slice of pizza from Ray's across the street simply had to be the first order of my New York day. As I walked into the restaurant the delicious smell of pizza instantly made my mouth water. All the different variations sitting behind the counter looked amazing.

"One slice please," I said pointing to a classic margarita.

"One slice of cheese pie for the Brit," the burly Italian American at the counter shouted back to his colleague with the same stature and tone.

This is the second time I ever heard pizza referred to as pie.

Pizza pie.

I LOVE IT.

A few minutes later a huge slice of pie arrived.

This *slice* which it was rather comically called (it was the size of a small pizza) covered every inch of the plate, all sides of the triangular slice hung deliciously around the over-worked cardboard. On the slice's arrival I was instantly reminded of the UK to USA portion sizes. Americans like to *go large*.

I paid Ray his money, and he promptly gestured to the opposite end of the counter where, if you're that way inclined, you had the option to add more cheese or some type of tired looking chilli pepper garnish.

I nodded to Ray, whilst making my way over, to the one thing I knew I would certainly need more of. Napkins. This was going to get messy!

(Whilst on the subject, I have to say I think most foods out there incorporating cheese and carbs are just trying to be pizza. Cheese on toast is an obvious pizza wannabe, I am telling you. Confused pizza.)

After all the sheer delights of breakfast food, there is nothing better than pizza when you're hungry, and boy was I hungry. I demolished Ray's generous slice and enthusiastically ordered another which followed the same speedy fate.

I washed it all down with a one-dollar cup of fizzy orange, or in American, Soda.

As always, I had my ice filled all the way to the top of the cup. Standard Pop.

After my dynamite meal I was back out on the street fully ready to go shopping. I promptly hailed a cab; I remember the driver's window finished opening the exact second the car stopped: this was clearly a technique honed by frequency.

"Where ya goin?" he hurriedly barked.

"Williamsburg please, mate," I responded with as much poshney as

I could possibly muster.

"Get in!"

I knew this move – an audition of sorts. I was 'in' this time. I've been 'out' plenty times before.

On the way to Williamsburg, we crossed the Brooklyn Bridge, from which I got a good old look of the Statue of Liberty. Although I had frequented the Big Apple numerous times, I'd never taken a moment to acknowledge the statue's stature. I regretfully commented to the driver that it looked 'much bigger' in the photos and videos. It's like London's Big Ben, not that big at all. It didn't go down too well, and I got shot the evil eye through the rear view mirror. Fair enough, I thought, I did straight up disrespect one of America's most prized monuments. The not so vibey moment between us quickly passed when the driver's attention shifted to loudly cussing out a fellow cabbie who cut him up.

"Screw you candy ass," he screamed.

I instantly tuned him out, and as the hostility continued between drivers, I went back to my wonderful window view and wished Pauly DiMaggio with his kind eyes and wicked humour was driving me instead. I was much more intrigued by the beautiful Brooklyn Bridge than the Statue of Liberty – bridges are often dazzling architectural feats and I do very much like to collect real life memories of my favourites.

My current top three are Tower Bridge in London, Sydney Harbour Bridge and you guessed it, Brooklyn Bridge. I wonder where in life we would be without bridges.

"A very great invention," I said to myself as Brooklyn Bridge ended and we hit the mainland. I was so inspired that later that same day I wrote in my diary:

(Diary extract)

Bridges! Bridges help us get to places. They join us to people. They are as wondrous as the invention of fire, telephone or the internet, there's no doubt about it, bridges are up there as one of the greatest inventions and connectors of human beings

It's a very Wonderboy type of thinking, I know. The exact type of musing I liked to scribble down for posterity.

I spent the rest of the journey sending a text to my Grandpa about some great clouds I saw flying over New York. He sent me a message back saying Grandma is making his favourite dinner, toad in the hole, with creamy cheddar infused mash (confused pizza) and mushy peas. Even his beloved clouds come second to his favourite meal cooked by his loving wife.

Soon enough we arrived in Williamsburg, and not long after that I was standing outside *THE TREASURE CLOSET.*

Treasures back then was a thrift store mecca on the cusp of excelling itself in the hipster cool premier league. NYC has always been noted for excellent thrift stores and flea markets, so my pre-arrival buzz was more than appropriate.

That day when I walked in I was instantly greeted with that familiar vintage musky smell and the sound of dancehall music, the drum beat and low-end bass sounded so good bouncing off all the vintage garments, all the rhythms helping dress the moment extra nicely, a great welcome and a most delightful start to my first ever Treasure Closet visit.

To say everything in that vintage chapel was incredible would be an understatement. It wasn't just a few special items you have to dig through racks and racks to reveal. Nope, everything was stellar. A big bouquet of fabulous.

I was clearly right at home as I was asked a number of times by fellow shoppers, "Do you work here?"

A compliment?

The shop was clearly made for me and my choice of attire, and I recall at the time regretting not withdrawing more *earth credits* from my post pizza ATM rendezvous!

That day it was hard not to notice the two small dachshund dogs running around the store. I am an animal person, they are all my friends, even the bears who scare the hell out of me, I don't discriminate, all creatures great and small are a friend of Pop's. Animals can tell the difference between those who have good vibes and those that don't so as soon as the dogs clocked me, they pitter-pattered their way over to hang out at my feet, trying to climb my legs like the intrepid explorers of the canine variety that they really were.

I politely asked their guardian, a tall red-headed lady with ironic tattoos and extreme gold hoop energy.

"What are the pups' names?"

"Nunya business!" she responded between loud smackie chewing gum chomps, clearly pleased with her spearminted sarcasm.

"It's like that then, is it?" I muttered with just enough volume she could hear my London tones with clarity.

"The golden one is VAN. The all-black one is HALEN," she responded without looking away from the heavily decorated rhinestone pink leather jacket she was perusing.

"A-plus for dog names," I chirped back, conscious of not taking up any more of her time.

I was up for a chat, but no dice.

I would have said how much that pink leather jacket suited her as I later saw her hesitantly hanging it back up on the revered vintage rack.

Regardless of all that, I was on my own mission. My new *garms* wouldn't be picking themselves. Within a very short duration, I had all I wanted, one metallic silvery bronze suit, a woolly poncho and a lumberjack style jacket with a light brown leather trim. After rummaging around at the bottom of a rack full of fake fur jackets, I found a small tartan suitcase with a nifty salmon pink inner lining. There was no price tag, but I assumed like everything else it was for sale.

With my brilliant thrifty items in order, I headed over to the cash register to purchase my bounty, the young man in charge even complimented me on my shopping choices.

"Why thank you, I bet you say that to all your customers," I responded.

His eyes widened as he placed my receipt into the small tartan suitcase along with the rest of my purchases.

"Shsssssssh, now you know my secret," he said with a good grin as he passed me my haul. This is when with his arm outstretched, I saw his DIY Black Flag tattoo. A DIY tattoo tells you a lot about a person.

"That's a wrap, jack. Have a great day now."

"Cheers, mate."

I was most pleased with my new acquisitions and couldn't wait to get back to try them all on. With that thought in mind I decided it was high time to head back to Casa Del Gershwin, and for an extra change of environment I would take the subway back into the city.

I got back to Manhattan fine but unfortunately and not surprisingly to the wrong borough completely.

To this day I still cannot understand how to navigate the New York City subway system. I genuinely think it's based on luck.

I'd been plenty lucky with my travelling since I left England and decided to not push it. I would instead walk back to the hotel, stretch the legs and all that. When I got up to street level, I and all the other emerging travellers were greeted to a drummer playing pots and pans at the very top of the station stairs. The lady was dazzling, beating the kitchen hardware in a unique carefree flow. A large crowd had quite rightly formed around this rhythmic wizardess, and I watched her for about twenty minutes before it started to rain, her trance broken only by the unusually large soft drops of rain falling from above and around the monstrous mountains of concrete and steel. When the drummer's pots and pans started filling up with water it promptly concluded the show.

"No encore tonight ladies and gentlemen," she announced before jumping up, gathering her makeshift instruments, and joining the heaving throngs heading down to the subway below and its welcome shelter from the elements.

As I made my way back to my temporary abode, I couldn't help thinking about the wizardess drummer. I hoped it would all go well for her and one day she could swap Canal Street station for Carnegie Hall.

The light had now finally faded for the day and the city evening began to gleam that cool New York City glow it's become so famous for. The rain reflecting off the shiny wet asphalt with occasional blasts of billowing steam from the gaps in the many manholes littering the roads is still an unforgettable memory of that moment.

Once I arrived back to the Gershwin, I began to ponder my special ability for losing hotel room key cards. It really is a talent I have.

"No problem," the smouldering lady at reception said whilst she cut me a new one followed by the offer of a warm complimentary chocolate chip cookie, and what I later discovered – her telephone number written on the card wallet holding the plastic multicoloured keycard.

Nice touch on the cookie Gershwin. My apologies Hannah: I lost your number as quickly as I lost my fruity new keycard.

Side note: a warm complimentary cookie used to be pretty standard in all American hotels upon check in. I had a field day when I first discovered this, the city was Boston, I believe the Doubletree hotel by the airport, it was our first ever coast to coast American tour. I fondly remember that zig zagging jaunt as I took the first bite of my warm gooey cookie.

Delicious.

AMERICA you're a glorious calorific maniac.

A very nice sugary high washed over me as I got back to my room. I was BUZZING. Perhaps it was the time difference, but I was bouncing off the walls. I needed to put this energy to good use, lucky for me I knew the exact activity.

Do you recall my rock and roll wigwams?

Well, what I didn't explain was the whole process was starting to become far more detailed, much more elaborate, or as my band mates would say, EXTRA. Whenever possible I was into rearranging whole hotel rooms.

To me, a good rearrange of a room was just like playing a song with the most beautifully sympathetic drumbeat.

Every beat in its most rightful and undeniable place – synergy!

I believe a hotel room, or any room with objects and furniture for that matter, should have that same natural synergy. When everything's in its optimum place you will find it accentuates what I call 'the natural vibrational power'. The Gershwin always had a good style, a nice natural vibrational power. Regardless of that I would still be compelled to move the bed to the opposite side of the room and reposition the desk, table, and chairs. It doesn't take long and as always, it's well worth it.

"Much better," I thought as I finished.

With my appetite suitably worked up, I began to flick through the room service menu, quickly concluding that Ray's pizza joint across the street felt far more appealing. After deciding my dinner plans, the massive American king size bed started looking at me funny. I didn't mind one bit that I had to remove an unending number of pillows and poofs before attempting to climb in. After all, in my mind this was how things are done in America – *the American way.*

After my pillow palaver, I began to get comfy and started reading a magazine article about a new water park in Dubai, something about the biggest river rapids ever built.

The edge of illegal was the phrase the journalist used to describe the attractions.

I love a good water park: *the edge of illegal* sounded perfect.

The next thing I remember is staring zombie-like into the TV. The Flintstones were on: the colours and old school vibes felt so nostalgic and wholesome. At some point I spotted in the corner of the room the small tartan suitcase laying on the electric mustard yellow armchair.

It was my *Treasure Closet* bounty. The sight filled me with an instant energy, and I decided there and then it was time to try on all my new *garms* again.

The room had a huge mirror which is essential for the fullest appreciation of such an occasion.

"Mega! I'll stick the kettle on."

Another fine example of why I loved the Gershwin. Kettles as standard in every room.

A kettle didn't seem to be a common thing in American hotels back then, although from my last few visits this does seem to have changed. It's still hard to make a good cup of tea though. You have to take your own bags for starters, something about the milk, something about the water, I don't know.

I drank peppermint tea back then. You could get good peppermint tea everywhere. I once met a Moroccan drummer from Marrakech who told me that peppermint tea in Morocco is drank as whisky is drank in Scotland. He said for religious reasons alcohol isn't desirable over there, so the next best thing took its place. I liked that, never forgot it.

So, with my steaming cup of Moroccan whisky in hand, I walked over to the armchair and picked up the small tartan suitcase. I then sat with it resting on my lap. It was a very handsome piece with lots of unusual hand stitched details. When I opened it up, I noticed for the first time that the shiny pink silky inner lining was worn away from its previous adventures. I could see that the damage was inside the top of the suitcase with the fabric frayed over time, exposing just enough to get a glimpse of what lay behind. You're not supposed to see this side of the suitcase. It's like going backstage at a concert, you're only supposed to see what's being presented, not necessarily what it takes to present it. My curiosity was insatiable though. I loved to see what was behind the curtain, and for better or worse I did what any Wonderboy would and carefully pulled back the shiny lining to take a good peep.

Straight away I noticed something unusual and further examination began immediately.

The hotel room had a standard light setting of *moody* so I re-positioned the suitcase below the dimmable floor lamp and promptly turned the dial to a setting called *stun*.

With the light set firmly to *stun* my hotel room was absolutely illuminated. It was now time to take another peek behind the shiny pink curtain. I didn't know what to expect, but being a Wonderboy the result isn't really the point, it's the potential for the unexpected that drives you. It was either intentional or accidental, but a secret compartment had been made and the contents had just been unwittingly discovered.

I proceeded to take everything out of the small suitcase and laid the contents on the floor around me. I then turned it upside down allowing gravity to deliver, what I think I had already glimpsed to my waiting hand below.

Dust and debris followed right behind a very old book.

I could feel that the material it was made from was old. It was also very worn, almost to the point of tattered. It felt rough and delicate to the touch. I handled it with great care! I even held the vintage book up to my nose and took a good curious sniff. I know it's strange but the impulse to do so was mighty.

I was most satisfied that I did.

Without sounding wet, the smell had a feeling of hope and ambition attached to it, like a crisp countryside morning or freshly baked bread.

It was a wholesome note.

A good vibe.

The book wasn't thick like the Bible or *Lord of the Rings*, it was more school-book size, light as a feather. I thought it might be someone's personal notebook or something like that, not a published piece of work.

"What type of book are you then?" I asked out loud, my words dusted with intrigue.

At this moment the Flintstones episode ended, as the adverts that followed were twice the volume of the cartoon, which instantly broke my attention. I got up, flicked the TV off and then opened the thick black out curtains. As I returned to my comfortable seated position, I thought to myself that a very unexpected turn of events had just occurred.

From the stainless steel, made-to-look-old clock hanging on the wall I could see it was almost 5am and with the city's glow slowly beginning to bounce around the room I went back to my discovery with vigour. I flicked through the book with an inquisitive eagerness, randomly picking a page to investigate further, the author's very neat handwriting revealing to me a short, sweet poem about a flock of birds in the summer sky flying in formation over New York City.

> *Come down and meet me at the station*
> *I feel the need to get away*
> *Are arms wide open in formation*
> *We'll fly together to better days*

The next page was a detailed pencil drawing of a very handsome house, written below in the same neat handwriting, *Home.*

The house looked like a dolls' house, something from a fairytale, with a wrap-around porch, detailed glass windows, which my Wonderboy imagination filled in as being stained glass of glowing reds and blues, in the garden the bushes, trees, flowers and shrubs looked carefully organised and luscious, I could see the house in my mind's eye, beautiful, stunning.

Every page was filled with stories or sketches.

There were hundreds of them, which I read back-to-back. To say I was completely immersed in the writing would be no exaggeration.

I connected with every word and phrase; every line of every drawing spoke to me. I was utterly consumed and as the heat of the new day's sun hit my face the glow finally engulfed the city's huge skyscrapers. With the fingers of light clawing their way through the once darkened metropolis, I looked up from the book to watch the sun finally finish rising in the reflection of a mirror-like building across the street. It felt symbolic, like my discovery was important and the sun coming up in this glorious manner was a confirmation of this special event.

With a smile on my face, I lovingly cradled the book, examining like a baboon inspecting its mate, which is when I noticed written on the spine of the book in exactly the same handwriting:

Property of Drewford Alabama

"Drewford Alabama, Drewford Alabama, Drewford Alabama," I repeated out loud like a scratched vinyl record stuck on loop. "What a name," I said.

I don't know how much time passed but at some point, I carefully wrapped the book inside a soft white Gershwin hotel towel and packed it away into my new tartan case. Of course, this time around the book would be travelling in the main compartment, first class! Then I sat back and rested my head on the soft cushioned headrest of the armchair and closed my eyes whilst massaging my temples gently. This was something I always saw Grandma doing when she was thinking deeply. I had adopted it from childhood, as I did, I thought about this Drewford Alabama. I was tingling with intrigue. Whoever they were I liked them immensely.

The thought moved seamlessly into me reliving the discovery of the book, it played back effortlessly, it was so vivid, even though it just happened I was actually taken aback by my ability to recall the moment with such clarity, I was even reliving it from a whole different perspective of looking down on myself from a bird's eye view of the Gershwin hotel room, I was going with it. It was cool.

So there I was observing myself lying in bed in the hotel room with my face glowing colourfully from the bright cartoon playing on the television. I watched myself notice the small tartan suitcase sitting on the armchair in the corner of the room. I smiled as I began to witness myself enthusiastically begin the process of getting out of bed to try on my new purchases. It was weird. I thought perhaps my temple rubbing had tapped me into some sort of meditative state which was helping me unlock some new potential mystical power within. It felt like it was worth my while hanging around to see where it went. I certainly wasn't planning to open my eyes!

All the events that occurred in my *real-life* memory of this moment continued to flow by with an HD-like quality. I watched as I look behind the shiny curtain of the tartan case and I see my face full of excitement when I get a glimpse of what was lying behind, the moment continues with me holding the book in my hands, pressing it against my nose for a good sniff then flicking through the pages just like I had done before, when out of nowhere something very new occurred.

Something that definitely didn't happen in my real-life memory of the moment.

It happened so quickly, but suddenly the book's writings and drawings vanished from the page as if they were written in invisible ink.

As all of this was happening I saw the reflection of me in the mirror, he (I) had a look of sheer disbelief across his (my) face. Then I watched with him (me) as a brand-new drawing began to emerge on the page.

It was as if it was being drawn in real time, no pen, no hand, just strokes and marks, dots and dashes all of which ended up in revealing a drawing of me.

Not just me I should add.

Me holding the very tattered old book!

Once the drawing was complete the invisible pen wielding hand began to speed up its charming speedy swirly handwriting, presenting me with.

HELLO ANDREW

Then continuing with two letters written one above the other:

Y

O

Just as both of us have time to acknowledge this mystical and downright spooky moment the writings disappeared, and all the original words and sketches returned. This is when I felt a tap on my shoulder. At first, I refused to turn around as I didn't want to miss anything from the view below. This tap continued and continued. It began to get harder and harder. It was only when the tap was teetering on sore that I eventually turned around to acknowledge the persistent vibe killer. As I did everything went black!

Later that day I was with Waldo my Irish friend with troubadourial tendencies.

We were hanging out ahead of our show later that night, chatting over some hot drinks we bought from one of the many overpriced java joints lining the New York streets.

"It was W I L D, man! Honestly, I felt like my Moroccan whisky had been spiked with hallucinogenics."

As I told Waldo all about my trippy experience, Waldo laughed. He laughed so much in fact his expensive coffee almost started coming out of his nose.

As his hysterics subsided, he chirped, "POP, your imagination is crazy, dude."

The damage was done though, his reaction was enough for me to decide there and then that if anything Drewford Alabama-esque was ever to happen again I should keep it firmly to myself. I then wrote down a few words reminding me of the whole surreal Drewford Alabama moment on the back of the coffee shop napkin.

Sketch of me holding book, Hello Andrew, Y, O,
Gershwin hotel room 613, Halloween, 1997.

Whatever had happened didn't feel over, discovering Drewford Alabama's book felt significant. And critically it felt most important that I shouldn't forget the drawing or mysterious message. Writing it down was almost second nature to me, without my trusty diary, the stained napkin would suffice. That's what was running through my mind as I folded the napkin into a little square and slid it into my back pocket.

"A little square of intrigue," I said out loud.

"What was that Pop?" Waldo asked.

"Nothing, mate," I muttered back.

Waldo and I then continued with our peachy swell New York day by going guitar shopping. All the guitars were far too expensive. Instead I ended up buying Waldo a red rhinestone gem guitar strap for our show in the evening. Waldo's favourite artist was Dolly Parton and it reminded us both of her. When Waldo wasn't looking, I bought it for him, I reckon the show's extra vibes that night were from Dolly's rhinestone presence!

The trip was a huge success. I avoided some incomprehensible downtime in London and my musical chops, as intended, got their refreshing change of scene, and a nice little workout to boot.

Win. Win.

After the show we drank cocktails and listened to old school rock and roll at a nearby dive bar, the type of place where the floors are sticky and you're glad it's barely lit. At some point it was decided food must be eaten and the Kitty Kat Diner a few blocks away on Bleeker Street would be the most ideal place to do so. It was time to water down the evening's sugary alcoholic beverages with some good old fashioned New York City deli food. Grilled cheese sandwiches, French fries and Coca-Colas all round.

The evening really couldn't get any better. I was so consumed with the music, the food and the general after-show frolics that I forgot all about Drewford Alabama's book and the whole weird trippy episode that came along with it.

It would be exactly two years to the day when Drewford Alabama would return to my thoughts.

PART TWO

The year – 1999

Location – Motorway

Mood – Quick

It was Halloween night and The Soho's were heading back to London from playing a show in Birmingham, home of Black Sabbath and the Peaky Blinders. The next day we were due to start a four-day recording session in a posh studio with a hip new producer with five different haircuts. Leading up to this point we had concluded that the only thing standing in the way of our ever-elusive success was having songs played on the radio.

The simple fact of the matter was the public at large were never going to hear about us unless we had what all the other bands doing better than us had. We knew without our songs rattling around in people's radios we would never be able to expand beyond our tiny loyal fan base.

Our solution was simple, we needed a HIT. Seems obvious, right?

Well not so much for us. We were children of the 70s, not in the sense of when we were born, but in the musical ethos of that era. A band back then could exist in a huge way just off the back of their musical prowess alone. Most often bands of that time would make three or four albums before their first hit ever even arrived, the band FREE or Bruce 'The Boss' Springsteen being great examples. The whole time their live shows got bigger and bigger, the sonic majesty alone carrying them to the stars and beyond. As long as your band was *smoking hot* you were all set for fame and glory.

Our songs could often go on for ten to fifteen minutes. We would bend and weave through the sections of music freely, whatever the feeling in the room or in our hearts, dictating where the songs went.

We could sing and play our instruments very well, so we always made the most of this musical freedom. We took our songs to any place we wanted and beyond. We then went right back around again and tucked you into bed. We never played our songs in the same way twice, which is very exciting if you are watching, but a harder prospect to pitch to the powers that be who hold the keys to the doors in the world of TV and radio. We needed these doors to be opened for us so we could rise up the ranks to the heights of success we craved so badly. All those miles we clocked up travelling around the world had started to feel real *long* and there was now no clearer message that we needed to *change our approach.*

In hindsight, I'm sure all the constant alcohol induced shenanigans that we were getting up to were contributing substantially to our unhealthy impatient mindset, but then again wasn't alcohol and drugs what all bands were supposed to do? Wasn't this expected of a gang of musical misfit pirates roaming the world?

I'd read all the books, seen all the movies, I mean, we've all heard the stories, right?

The only thing missing from our picture was the roar of thousands. The thing is for us the shows were actually beginning to get in the way of the partying. Never a good sign. I look back at all this and realise it was just our way of dealing with the unspoken disappointment that we were all starting to feel about our lack of progress in the popularity department. Things were getting out of hand, and it felt most appropriate to apply all our energies into writing songs, catchy songs, songs that could be played on the radio.

How hard could that be?

Soon enough every spare moment was used to write.

Sound checks. Hotel rooms. I have a fond memory of being posted up in a Seattle motel writing songs late into the night by a teardrop-shaped, turquoise lit swimming pool.

All the bedrooms overlooked the pool and soon enough an audience gathered which naturally led us to an impromptu performance for a dozen or so folk.

(Diary extract)

I will never forget the smell of honeysuckle flowers and chlorine mixed in the air
of that warm Seattle night at the Phoenix hotel. For a moment I was
transported. I imagined that I was in the 70s and the pool was part
of one of those old Hollywood Hills rock star houses.

I drifted off whilst playing. That musical drift off is a magical place, the point
where you're just letting the music tell the story, no conscious effort required,
just a constant reaction to what's happening around you.

I think the best music is created in this state, hang on a second,
is jazz built on these musical reactions?

I know. Proper Wonderboy vibes.

The pool side show ended when Maz our Brazilian rock star front woman in a supreme showbiz climax executed a flawless backflip off a deck chair into the water, which prompted everyone else watching to follow suit – me and our multitasking guitarist Vic included.

Our sonic vibrations had made this joyous occasion of bringing once complete strangers together by the power of song, everyone sharing the same magnificent moment at the exact same time: simply magical.

With such focus and determination in the song writing sweepstakes we soon had well over 100 compositions, each and every single one of them written with the intention of being a hit.

Predictable, but deliciously so.

Turns out we were rather capable at this task, because when we put our minds to it, we found we were really good at *catchy*. No guitar or drum solos here. No ten-minute improvised interlude sections before you hit your first chorus. Nope, we had been there and done that and it got us nowhere.

There's a phrase I recently heard: DON'T BORE US. GET US TO THE CHORUS!

Well, even we got bored. It was now time for a wardrobe change, and baby we were going disco. We wanted ten songs for our new album, so by the law of averages there was bound to be a hit buried in that bag of songs somewhere.

To me they all were smashers, but I was obviously massively biased. It would turn out I wasn't alone in my hit ratio estimation, as it was agreed by all who heard our big bag of songs that we had exactly what it would take for us to get to where we wanted to go.

Things were different for us now. We had amicably parted ways with Cynthia who was retiring for the second and final time in her life. She was already in her late 60s when she first started managing the band. We loved Cynthia and were sad to see her go, but she was adamant that we now needed someone new, someone fresh and fiery and as her parting gift she got us signed up with Hit Machine management, one of the biggest music management companies in the world. All we needed now was the right producer for our new sound and the four-day recording session we were driving through the dead of Halloween night to make was exactly that: a touch of record producer courting.

Hit Machine didn't want us jumping into bed straight away with the first famous producer who showed us attention. We had the songs and word about town was we had hits.

You learn in this business that the more people who want to work with you, the more likely you're doing something right.

Sure, all the attention was flattering, but in my opinion, *about bloody time.*

The main thing was we were moving forwards, moving into uncharted territory. It was just what we needed. We were ready to *go baby go.* So that night it was already decided that I would be last to be dropped off home aka Benji the trust fund cowboy's gaff. Sometimes I would be first, sometimes second, that night last, no problem, all good.

As Rosie turned off Belsize Park Gardens on to Harbour Road, the blue flashing lights and roadblocks greeting us were the most alarming 4am sight indeed.

Swiss army Eddie our tour manager slash sound engineer slash guitar tech had moments before he lit a huge joint and instantly thought it was all to do with him and his medical grade reefer – his Ganja paranoia was not playing around these days – but I was far too concerned with what was going on down my road to assure him otherwise.

"Stop here mate. I'll get out."

As I got out of Rosie the first thing I noticed was the air. It was filled with acrid smoke which you could instantly taste at the back of your throat, I coughed and spluttered as I walked down the street passing countless fire engines and ambulances blocking my view making it impossible to work out what the hell was going on up ahead.

My watery eyes and runny nose gave the whole tense scenario an extra layer of WHAT THE FUCK!

Our house was at the very end of the street and the further I walked down towards it the more I got the feeling something really bad had gone down with my neighbours… It didn't for a second occur that any of this fuss could be to do with me.

As soon as I saw Benjy and his on/off girlfriend Alicia sitting on the curb in their matching his and hers Gucci pyjamas my heart sank.

As I passed the final police van impeding my view, I got a good look at where I lived, Benjy's house, which now had no roof, all the windows smashed out and garish black burn marks completely covering the scorched brickwork of *OUR* once dysfunctional but happy home.

"Benjy, what the fuck, are you ok?" I asked.

Benjy frustratingly just laughed.

"The house got burnt Pop. It's not a problem. I'll get another one."

He said this, without even looking up from the racing game he was playing on his phone.

"Not a problem?"

My tone seemed to help him understand the potential severity of the situation as he briefly looked up to access the calamity, before once again returning to his game.

"Was anyone hurt?"

"Nah," Alice responded matter-of-factly.

As another trust-fund kid, this casual response was typical of both their enormous out-of-touch-with-reality lives.

Luckily that night it transpired everyone was out, but the two inter-mittent love birds, who it seemed had fallen asleep whilst watching an old Elvira vampire flick, they got out just in time when the fire alarms kicked off and a thick noxious smoke filled the house.

"It all happened so quickly," Alicia said.

"They were lucky to get out alive," a skulking baby-faced Bobbie on the beat chipped in.

The policeman needed Benjy to sign his report, but Benjy was oblivious. All he wanted to do was play his game. In his world there wasn't an issue, he would just buy a new house, problem solved. Even the baby-faced police officer and his request for attention and cooperation was a major inconvenience to Benjy.

Rich people's issues.

From what I saw the house was completely destroyed, and as my initial shock wore off, I remember beginning to feel just like Benjy. I didn't care, no one was hurt which in itself was an absolute miracle and all my possessions could be replaced.

When the police were finished and all necessary papers signed, we were finally allowed to leave.

I ended up getting a lift with the two lucky-to-be-alive trust fund kids to the hotel Benjy's dad owned on central London's exclusive Park Lane. He never liked to talk about this place but after a few drinks he always did, he resented it, despised is possibly a better word. Benjy felt the hotel got more attention and love than he ever did as a kid and from this I believe the lad never recovered.

Benjy had a heart of gold and, when I think about it now, I believe it was his heavy heart that always kept him struggling to stay above the water. From what he said the rest of his family were cold folk; his siblings were much more like their father. I even got the impression Benjy was possibly a bit of an embarrassment to them all: his lack of desire for power was not in theme with their way of life.

I zoned out on the journey from North London to Park Lane, snapping back to reality in the reception of the fancy hotel at the exact moment Benjy told a silver-haired man, who called Benjy 'Sir Benjamin', to book me into one of the penthouse apartments. Benjy and Alicia took another. We'd gone from housemates to neighbours. The three of us shared a glass elevator up to the top floor where we hugged and said our goodbyes. It would be the last time I saw either of them.

My penthouse was, as you can imagine, total five-star lavish elegance.

Spread over two floors with a games room, including novelty no cash required vintage arcade machines, a terrace with hot tub, sauna, barbecue with decked out seating area all centred around a large jade stone cherub water fountain shooting a curved arrow of aqua into an all-glass koi carp fish pond. Continuing with its palatial qualities, what about the movie room with popcorn machine and sofa size cinema seats? Or the choice of three bedrooms, all with movie star size ensuite bathrooms? The place even came with its very own butler named 'Presley' on call at a moment's notice.

In a smoky blink of an eye, Pop had gone high class.

The evening couldn't have been crazier. After I finished inspecting my new digs, I decided to sit outside under the clear central London sky, with the sound of water flowing from the chunky cherub and the comfy deck chair. I already felt at home and nestled in. I sat and pondered the insane events of the night. I rubbed my temples and felt any tension I had leave me. It was in this peaceful state that everything that happened on the night I discovered Drewford Alabama's book returned.

It all came back to me and, like before, it was just as vivid. I was very aware I was sitting out on the terrace in my Park Lane penthouse, yet I really felt like I was also back in New York City, looking down on myself from my aerial vantage point inside the hotel room. Just like before, I was afraid to open my eyes for fear of losing the moment.

I watched as I switched on the television and the familiar cartoon and its theme tune filled the room with bright colourful light and song. I see myself acknowledging the tartan suitcase and its damaged lining, and I watch my reaction as I turn it upside down to allow the beaten-up old book to fall into my awaiting hand below. The dream was identical until the very end where the book's contents disappear, and that ghostly invisible hand once again began writing again only this time it was a completely different message from before.

As all of this was unfolding, I began to feel myself being shaken back and forth, rocking gently at first, just like being a passenger in a rowing boat on a wavy sea, until it started to get progressively more intense, something more akin to being a rag doll in the hands of an overstimulated child.

I endured this persistent pushiness until the ghostly invisible hand finished writing, only then did I look away to see what was causing the aggressive to-ing and fro-ing. The moment I tried to catch a peep of the culprit everything went black.

The next thing I knew I woke up lying on the sofa pillows arranged in the huge living area space. I had no memory of setting up one of my rock and roll wigwams. It was a poor attempt, not even a bed sheet roof.

I was slightly sore but very thrilled that my mystery Drewford Alabama had returned.

Sitting up I took a moment to gather myself before I thought about Grandpa's 'dreams are like oranges' analogy. His vibes gave me all the inspiration I needed to move over to the desk where the hotel room pen and paper was located, and just like before on the back of a napkin in the Greenwich village coffee shop, I scribbled down the new message:

YOU FOUND ME

Followed by another two seemingly random letters presented one above the other.

U

H

As I wrote I could feel my upper body muscles tight and strained, and thought nothing of it. It comes with the territory of being a ferocious drummer, from time to time the drums bite back. I certainly didn't think my rag-doll-dream-effect had anything to do with it. Plus, I'd gone hard in Birmingham the night before. I even ended up doing an impromptu drum solo – it was Maz's idea. I think she wanted a break to change outfits – that was the only cue I needed to hear to tear it up. You give me a glimmer and I will take a mile. It was going great until my drum sticks broke but got greater when I ended up playing with just my hands, thrashing away in a tsunami-like wave of rhythm.

"An unstoppable force," Vic said to me after the show. Vic was always great for complimenting you if you did something extra special. He had ears like a hawk has eyes.

I decided to go back to bed, only this time I used one of the traditional bedrooms, the nearest one to me. Lying fully awake in my new 5-star queen size bed my mind was working overtime. I couldn't stop thinking about Drewford Alabama and the events of the previous night. As these fiery thoughts ran through my mind, I became transfixed by a hairline crack in the electronically controlled blinds which was sending a sharp clean blade of sunlight right through the centre of the room. I could see tiny flecks of dust reflecting in the beam as they floated through the vibrant glow.

I was just acclimatising to the new day when two things struck me:

One, dust doesn't discriminate does it? And two, I'd totally changed my mind from the night before.

I *did* care.

I cared immensely as the mysterious Drewford Alabama book just happened to be somewhere within Benjy's fire-ravaged house, now without doubt burnt to a crisp with everything else. I was gutted, mortified, angry! I felt close to tears. I had no idea I felt so strongly about Drewford's Book. Lying there in all of that Park Lane luxury, I realised it was unlike everything else I owned – absolutely irreplaceable – and I was thoroughly devastated that it was gone forever. Although I must say this devastation was dispersed surprisingly quickly when I heard a collection of spritely taps on my door.

Room service. Brekkie time.

Drewford Alabama temporally left my thoughts as I got my food.

By the way, I had ordered every single item on the menu and became semi-embarrassed when multiple trolleys had to be put into action to bring this greedy drummer his orders.

I would eat almost everything.

Almost.

I left just one croissant for example. I did this because I thought if I left one thing it would show some sort of self-restraint, like the insane amount of food I just inhaled wouldn't be considered far too much for one person.

I did mention I struggled with my weight, right?

You can see why.

Moderation is what I lacked, especially when it came to the taste bud department. It was never food's fault though, just my inability to control the urge to taste more. It was always like that with the things I loved the most. In some instances, that was a good thing, like practicing obsessively for instance: that only made me a better musician and a better band member.

But eating obsessively, or even simply not watching what I eat, would always make me fat, and being fat was not the type of image I was seeing around with the other bands. I was in the entertainment industry after all.

I know when we first moved to Hit Machine management, they were 'concerned' with my historical 'fluctuating' size. They wanted us to know that they preferred the smaller Pop and offered to get me in touch with a personal trainer.

Within the inner circle of our band, I made a point of finding all of this absolutely hilarious, yet inside it struck a raw nerve, like what I feared when I was growing up watching MTV, seeing all the skinny drummers in the videos and realising I was not like them. It was a kicker all over again.

I had never really dealt with my size properly. The methods to combat my often-uncontrollable feeding frenzies would either be not eating again that day and starving myself into feeling less guilty, or the messier, more time-consuming method of sticking fingers down my throat and throwing up. It never really felt in vogue to discuss this subject before, but of course men suffer here too. We don't like to talk of these things, I think it's because without knowing, it has been subtly programmed into us as kids to keep schtum, like there's an archaic, boys-to-men code that must be followed, otherwise you're not considered a proper lad, a real man. Let me just say *fuck that!*

Around this time, I was on a good wave. I was looking great, the slenderest I had been in years. It was more of a product of playing and partying every night than healthy living but that didn't bother me in the slightest. A result is a result.

So after my breakfast I got ready to leave for the studio by using the jacuzzi bath in one of my plush bathroom options, I squeezed a whole miniature bottle of bubble bath and just lay there in the XXL soaker tub for a soothing sandalwood perfumed hour until my hands turned pruney and the smell of smoke was finally banished from my hair and skin.

As it's the usual order of things after the bath I got dressed. I don't usually do this but that day I slicked my hair back using a blob of very nicely fragranced hair conditioner to hold it all in place.

I enjoyed changing up my style like this, it's just like playing different genres of music with lots of different people. It keeps you fresh.

The hotel had washed my indigo-coloured dinner trousers and procured a fancy collarless black linen shirt which suited me mighty fine, and despite the previous evening's inferno I felt most excellent.

The five-star hospitality was on fire like my old home (I couldn't help myself) and bar my missing book, the fiery day's events were old news in Pop Morrison's world.

Thank you. Next.

Before heading off to the studio I thought about the recent cryptic Drewford Alabama message written on the notepad in the master bedroom.

I stopped at the double door entrance to my ludicrous new digs, waited for a couple of seconds then reached the conclusion that I couldn't leave it behind. I promptly retrieved the handwritten paper which I then tucked away into the front pocket of my leopard print rucksack. The front pocket was reserved solely for special things of this nature, amongst these sentimental items – a lucky shiny black stone shaped like a heart, a lucky gold chain with an owl pendant and a lucky peacock feather I found when last visiting my grand-parents. My instincts already deemed these dreams to be precious, so I felt the scribbled paper definitely belonged there amongst all my other special things.

When I left the hotel that day I didn't think about the book or dream again, I went about my days and weeks oblivious to anything that didn't directly relate to the band.

The producer with five haircuts who we were auditioning worked out beautifully so we extended our recording session from four days to six weeks.

Sometimes you gotta just strike when the iron's hot, right?

Benjy felt guilty about me now being technically homeless, so he extended his invitation for me to stay in the hotel as long as I wanted. I didn't get to keep the pimped-out penthouse. I moved a few floors down. I still had the money shot Hyde Park view and room service on the house. I was spoilt rotten!

Life carried on as normal. Normal being far from it, but normal for me.

I had everything I needed and more. I was living for free in luxury while making my second album with a famous producer and an excited record label who would be putting all their industry weight behind us upon the record's release.

It hadn't been talked about amongst the band, but it felt like there was something at stake. Before we had no one to prove anything to but ourselves, there were no expectations but our own which despite the lack of commercial success, musically I would still call a win. This was different though, now we needed to prove to everyone who supported us they were right, and prove to those who didn't they were wrong. We wouldn't allow our band to be yet another major label failure that couldn't even get out of the starter blocks – no way – we wanted to have our cake and eat it. Personally, I wanted double and triple portions, my hunger was insatiable, and cake is all I would accept.

Besides this ever looming and self-created pressure the studio sessions were going incredibly well and after spending all my creative and mental energies in the lab each day, I would return to my fancy hotel room at night and watch TV and order room service until I fell asleep. One night I got back to my room to find a parcel wrapped in tin foil on my bed.

How curious I thought as I opened the small envelope sellotaped to the weird aluminium parcel.

POP, THEY SAID THAT THIS IS THE ONLY THING THAT
SURVIVED THE FIRE. IT'S YOURS MATE.
BENJY.
PS I didn't have any wrapping paper

I ripped open the tinfoil wondering what could possibly have survived that fire. Benjy had sent me some photos the police took a week after the blaze, the place was destroyed, completely decimated. The house was condemned and was going to be knocked down.

I felt like the little boy who discovered the golden ticket in the chocolate bar when I saw what lay within. Underneath four layers of tin foil was a very large sweetie tin my lovely but very strange uncle had bought for my seventh birthday.

I instantly roared with laughter.

Was I really that happy about a reunited sweetie collection?

I really like sweets, but no, of course not.

It was what I had put inside the tin that got me so gassed.

After the original sweets had been consumed (which was in no time at all) it promptly became the hiding spot for all my important possessions that wouldn't be travelling with me on the road. I pulled the lid off the tin eagerly, I could see my birth certificate, driving license, money from different countries, a selection of marbles that didn't really belong there and hiding below all of this, wrapped tightly inside a soft Gershwin hand towel was Drewford Alabama's book, the book I once thought I would never see again.

Me and the book stayed together for a whole year in the hotel before I lost track of it again.

Year – 2003

Mood – Elation

Company – La Familia

Location – Worldwide

A week after our album W, I, L, D, was released I woke up with end-less missed calls and voicemails. I only listened to one message. It was from Cynthia Andrews our old manager,

> *Pop, it appears you have a hit record on your hands.*
> *Congratulations you three. You all truly deserve this.*

I just stared out the window. My initial emotion was straight relief, followed shortly by joy, pure joy! As intended our second album was released to much fanfare and applause. The true litmus test for any successful album is always how it lands with the public, not the labels, managers, or PR teams. Our album passed with flying colours and upon its release it immediately flew up the charts.

Perhaps flew up the charts is the wrong choice of words, it in fact sky-rocketed all the way to the top, crushing all those it passed. It couldn't have come at a more timely fashion and, oh boy, oh boy did we party – the ecstatic platinum delirium went on for days and days – possibly weeks!

At some point during the partying Maz's tattoo artist boyfriend turned up, who just so happened to bring his work along with him: a black metal toolbox with punk rock stickers like NOFX and Green Day stuck all over it. Of course, the plethora of permanent inks and tattoo guns were out in no time and the alcohol-infused tats were dished out as freely as everything else.

I was the only tattoo-less band member, which wasn't for a dislike of tattoos or anything like that, just a mixture of not getting round to it and never knowing what to get. That night I was drunk enough on Long Island ice teas to decide, when I saw Albee hovering above a glossy red-letter box on the street outside, that he was my spirit animal and I should honour that symbolic fact with ink.

I got the small blackbird tattooed on my inner right arm about the size of one of those complimentary boxes of matches you always used to get in hotel bars.

Everyone said the tattoo wouldn't hurt but it did. It hurt like hell. Once it was done, I forgot all about it, that would have been down to the more illicit party supplies taking their full effect, that and the buzz of basking in our long awaited and eagerly accepted accomplishment.

All our hard work had paid off.

This was the big time, it was certified, we were at top of the food chain, joining those illustrious ranks, it was *La Familia*.

Literally overnight our lives changed.

We had songs all over the radio and finally our tour posters had that all-important SOLD-OUT banner I once craved so badly, printed across them. We had finally arrived and with it came that previously missing roar of thousands. Such a sweet sound.

We now had fans. Lots and lots of beautiful fans.

We were Coca-Cola famous.

With this success all aspects surrounding the business of being a band were given a new lease of life. Huge shows, television appearances, radio appearances, interviews, red carpets, photoshoots, meet and greets, the list goes on. Doors opened for us that we never knew existed and overnight we were thrust into a whole new world. Fancy A list parties, film premieres, signing autographs, even turning on high street Christmas lights.

We were doing it all.

That seems to be how quickly things change in this music game: it's extraordinary, and a complete and utter mind-fuck.

I took every opportunity offered, and then went back again as always intended for seconds and thirds. I can't lie. I let it all go properly to my head. I felt like nothing could touch me.

Living in the fast lane began to feel very normal very quickly. I was playing the best drums in the very best venues and making records that lots of people loved listening to. It was every type of exciting.

Something you can never really take into account for though, is all the other things that come with reaching that highest rung on the entertainment ladder. I had quickly exceeded all my goals and dreams, I was now 'riding the gravy train,' to a destination unknown.

I moved from my Park Lane hotel room to an equally beautiful and luxurious marble floored, all-glass and sandstone-walled penthouse with panoramic views of the great city of London sitting right by the glorious River Thames, a muscular stone's throw away from Tower Bridge.

Pop's Palace, as Vic and Maz called it, was my new extremely indulgent, extravagant, utterly plush home. The nickname was most appropriate.

I wasn't going to set up rock and roll wigwams in this place; there would be no painting behind the paintings here.

I had a spacious master bedroom with private balcony and official prints by all my favourite artists' work lining my walls, artists like Salvador Dali, Keith Haring, Jackson Pollock, and Jean-Michel Basquiat.

The place was fit for a rock star. Perfect for me!

I loved the open plan layout of the place. The sunken *conversation pit* area in the centre of the main living area with its very own purple velvet wrap-around sofa surrounding a toasty 360-degree smokeless fireplace was a really nice detail from the Swedish architect who designed the place. I interpreted it as a tip of the hat to the cocaine cowboy cities like Miami during the 70s although I am completely sure it would have only been me and a handful of others who shared that same heady comparison.

The fireplace was fully controllable with a remote, in fact everything was fully controllable with a remote, windows, curtains, music, lights, it went on and on, I had trays of the things. It was a feature the estate agent seemed very keen to highlight.

Me, I don't mind getting up to turn the light switch off or open a curtain.

The architect must have been a foodie as the kitchen was a sleek marvel to behold, a classy touch was the hob sitting slap bang in the centre of the kitchen on a spacious solid granite island making it possible to cook and entertain guests at the same time, it's also something the remote-happy estate agent highlighted when I came to visit for the first time. She called the kitchen *highly functional, ideal for the entertainer.*

I was sold hook, line, and sinker on *ENTERTAINER.*

"I'll take the place!"

The kitchen would be wasted on me though as the most I ever made there was tea and toast.

To continue with me living large at *Pop's Palace,* I must mention my fully stocked bar with cocktail umbrellas and mini guitar shaped ice cubes, fine wines, luxury liquors and most importantly, Guinness on tap.

I recall one half-cut night, after drinking endless pints of the famous Irish drink, ordering myself four huge 65-inch plasma television screens from the home shopping channel. I forgot all about these drunk purchases, as I quite often did with such inebriated impulse buys. I was most surprised when the building's concierge Big George rang up one day to notify me of their arrival. He brought them up later, along with a handyman and electrician I'd asked him to procure to install them all.

Big George was a gentle giant of a man, a cockney through and through, with hands as rough as a week-old French baguette. I shook his hand only once to find this out. It was fist bumps from that day onwards.

The televisions would turn out to be completely wasted on me as I only ever watched the one in the bedroom. The others hung on the sandstone walls like dark flat oblong windows looking into a pitch-black parallel universe, which is how I began to think of them anyway. The TVs would still be considered one of the good drunk purchases I made. The good ones are really easy to remember as they were very few and far between. For example, I bought a ton of shares in a Californian weed farm and a ride-on lawn mower the size of a small car for Grandpa and Grandma.

Like I say, good purchases.

Bad buys were frequent and varied dramatically in badness from a very expensive dinosaur bone that turned out to be made from papier-mâché and a white grand piano which arrived in a shoe box which was far bigger than it needed to be. Turns out it was a toy for a dolls house, but it looked massive in the pictures. I wondered why it was so cheap. I thought I'd found a bargain!

I'd even got myself an original vintage and rare jukebox that I rescued from The Dolphin, my local pub. It was a sign of the times. They were modernising – MP3s, Bluetooth and uploading was in, dusty old jukeboxes out. I filled it with all my favourite bands' records, including of course, my own. The absolute proof of luxury-living though was the private elevator. I even got to pick the accompanying elevator music. The song? 'Riders on the Storm' by The Doors. With its long intro you never got to hear Jim Morrison sing, but that didn't matter as the rainstorm and optimistic organ riff with expert accompanying bass playing and drumming was the most fabulous mood setter to soundtrack the twenty-five second journey to and from.

If I was throwing a party, it would be 'Here Comes the Hotstepper' by Ini Kamoze.

I didn't know what I was doing. I was out of control. It should have been AC/DCs 'All Night Long'. Angus Young's legendary guitar riff could revive an Egyptian mummy.

My new home's fellow residents were a mixed bunch who I rarely saw, a few TV personalities, a movie star or two, some plastic surgeons, a footballer and a dodgy rich son of a Russian oligarch who'd been unsuccessfully 'evicted' from the building on the grounds he posed a 'serious risk' to fellow residents and the building itself. Whatever went on with this crazy cat happened way before my time. I would later learn shooting guns from his various balconies had something to do with it, and it turns out it's extremely difficult to evict a billionaire's kid with their own security detail.

For me it was all rather outrageous, and I would often think to myself, 'Of course I live here. This is how all famous drummers live, ain't it?'

I thought about buying a fancy sports car, but realised I loved being driven around far more. I also thought that removing the driving aspect from my responsibilities would give me lots more time to indulge in my brand new rockstar party lifestyle.

I would go on extravagant holidays, hang out with the coolest people, and eat at the fanciest restaurants, the type of places with hip names like 'Catch' or 'Hyde,' where the food is served on pieces of wood, spades or other things of that nature and the portions are minuscule and always presented with colourful dots and dashes of foamed beetroot or carrot. After you have taken your standard 'wow that's pretty' camera snaps, I found the food would disappear off the plate way too quickly. It was never enough for a 'growing' lad like me. These places were always more about the environment, the service, the high-end factor. I loved the whole experience. However, I would always end up at a fast-food joint later in the night. Once again, it's all about greed really, that and everything in-between.

I was basically doing exactly whatever the hell I wanted, whenever the hell I wanted, and more often than not I was being an absolute obnoxious twat about it all.

I can admit that easily now. Try telling me that back then though! Wowza.

I felt untouchable. I was wild and free, spending money like I had a machine printing it in a back room.

I loved the madness that surrounded it all, the whole *hoo-ha* about being in a famous band was a complete thrill. Of course I was semi-aware of the cringy cliched reality of it all, but the fact was I was a fiend for the rock star lifestyle, it suited all my character traits immensely, like jam in a doughnut.

Something that never got old for me was entering a room to the whispers.

"Oh look, that's Pop the drummer." I always got a real kick out of that.

I loved being bounced to the front of queues, all the free clothes, gadgets, and events I was gifted or invited to. It's what I call rare air, a different life and subsequently I was nurturing a rather sizeable ego from it all, the extra attention was going to my head, never a good thing for a young fiery drummer with a hit record and a fat wallet. To go along with my new glittery position in life I had my very own celebrity girlfriend.

Libby Wynstanley presented the band with an album of the year award at one of those glitzy media-heavy ceremonies on a huge boat moored in Chelsea Harbour. From that night on, every time I went out, we would bump into each other. It's not like we 'just clicked'. I believe coincidence and circumstance brought us together far more than tangible chemistry. We both suited each other's lifestyles, a one-time morning radio personality turned daytime TV fixture with aspirations of being a movie star: Libs, like me, loved the fast life. Cocaine, champagne and the celebrity sport of ladder climbing were her hobbies, short dresses and fur jackets her uniform.

Libby's blonde bob with trademark cherry red lipstick and dark-smudged eyes set against her freckled olive-toned skin always attracted double takes from passersby. She had a temptress movie star look about her; it's just a shame acting wasn't her forte. This is something of a confirmation for me that talents don't necessarily always get passed down in the old gene pool. Both Libby's parents were hugely successful actors: her dad was one of the longest serving characters in a dreary multi-decade running TV soap and her mother focused all her talents in theatre and the occasional reoccurring role in a mega movie franchise about magic.

Libs and I looked great together and the paparazzi loved to snap us rolling out of clubs, S-class vehicles, or coming and going from whatever event we were attending.

If we were in the papers, I would be duly informed by my grandparents who collected every press clipping that ever mentioned me. They recorded every TV and radio show the band appeared on. They often knew more about my whereabouts than I did. I have a very strong memory of one of their calls. I'd just got back home from a short promo run up and down the country. Our mission had been to visit all the regional radio stations who were playing our records, a quick chat accompanied by an acoustic rendition of our latest hit was the order of the day. This was a typical 'you scratch our back, and we'll scratch yours' type of scenario, one of which I was happy to take part in if it helped sustain us or make our band even bigger.

I will never forget what happened when I got home. As the lift doors to Pop's Palace slid expensively open and I walked into the entrance foyer to my home, I was instantly greeted with one of my prized platinum discs hurtling past my head and smashing against the wall behind me. The barrage of abuse accompanying the flying disc was coming from Libby, who for reasons unknown, was beyond angry.

Fortunately, I was saved by the bell, my mobile telephone started vibrating in my pocket – it was Grandma.

Nothing ever got in the way of me speaking to Grandma, certainly not another ding-dong with my missus. Without hesitation, I walked straight through the penthouse to the master bedroom as far away as possible from the enraged girlfriend and promptly locked the door behind me. That only solved half the problem as I could still hear Libby smashing up my possessions in the other rooms, a most distracting and un-ideal backdrop for talking to my precious Grandma. My solution was to step out onto the balcony, and once I slid the huge industrial glass doors shut behind me sweet silence ensued, I finally answered the phone. As I did, I looked up to the sky and saw it was completely shrouded in full fat dark menacing Mammatus clouds – that day was a stormy type of day in every sense of the word. All that dissipated the moment I heard Grandma's voice.

"Hey Grandma, how are you?"

Without any greeting Grandma was straight to business.

"We are fine love. You know you were in the Sunday papers again? Gosh Libby's a bonnie lass sure enough. I just think she needs to wear more clothes. She's going to catch herself a death of a cold."

Bonnie lass. That was Grandma showing off her proud Scottish roots right there.

CRASH, SMASH, RIP, BANG!

I could still hear the bonnie lass herself continuing to smash up the gaff. I guess she'd found the key to the bedroom and was now working her way around my inner sanctum. Pop's Palace was getting a proper hiding.

"Yes, Grandma, I'm sure she can wear more clothes. I'll mention it."

I never would though. Libby's beauty equalled her temper – something I was just beginning to discover the extent of. Questioning her clothing choice would not end well, and in truth Libby's attire was A-okay with me. I liked her sultry clad swagger a lot. That was her style, she came that way. Besides, there was this mutual unspoken feeling that our relationship was good for business, no change was necessary. If it ain't broke, don't fix it.

I moved swiftly past the controversial subject of skimpy clothing by talking about clouds.

"There's strong Mammatus clouds overlooking London today, Grandma. Tell Gramps, he would love them."

Grandma and I went on to talk up a storm, just long enough for the storm kicking off inside my home to calm down. As always, I signed off our conversation with lots of love and good vibrations. After Grandma hung up, I went back inside to discover what the hell had stirred Libby up so destructively.

The reason for her smashy-smashy grievance?

Fruity business of the highest order!

It turned out she thought I was cheating on her when she saw some text messages going back and forth between her bestie Nancy and myself. Libby immediately took that to mean cheating was at play when in fact Nancy and I were in cahoots planning a surprise for Libby in the shape of a party to celebrate her landing a role in some film about robots or aliens, perhaps robots *and* aliens – something like that. I never saw it, no one did in fact, the film was pulled due to licensing issues before it even got released. Me and Nancy hired a bowling alley, and an award-winning Spice Girls cover band. Everyone but Sporty looked and sounded bang on!

Boy was Libby sorry when I set her straight. I was so pissed off I asked her to leave, actually I didn't even ask. I threw her phone and handbag in the elevator and hurled the universally accepted "Fuck off!" as a prickly goodbye into her general vicinity, while loading up two pop tarts into my brand new 'gifted' pink toaster. In the following calm I inhaled my tarty treats on the balcony just before the dark fluffy Mammatus started leaking.

The rain was temporary, very much like our argument because only a few days later the band would be heading off on a private jet to a billionaire's private island to use a recording studio in return for playing a few songs at the daughter's birthday party. Thrown in on the deal was a hundred grand each and a two-week island holiday.

Hell yes!

I decided to bring Libby and three of her equally smoking-hot girlfriends and together we all painted the island in sparkly glittery red. And naturally no band work was done. I don't think anyone even set foot in the studio!

What happened was Libby and I re-connected massively, and it started to feel like there were some real love shaped feelings flourishing between us. We went from 'fisty cuffs' to 'could this be love?'

This was a snapshot of life back then.

Lifestyles of the rich and famous.

On paper it couldn't be better.

Here's the thing: all that glitters is not gold. After all my dreams coming true, all the success we achieved, never once did it feel enough, and never once was my thirst ever fully quenched.

Jamie Morrison

(Diary extract)

Why am I always left wanting more, more, more?
Why is it that every time I get more, more, more I'm left feeling unsatisfied?
What's wrong with me?

Working hard and staying busy is a great sedative, and for a while it was enough to dull my bewilderment on why I wasn't content. Eventually too much time passed, and it became impossible to avoid the fact something was amiss, yet I pretended to feel happy because frankly, how could you not be?

What to do?

I'm sort of embarrassed to say this now, but I carried on exactly the same, it was all about more, more, more!

The Date – 2004, October 22nd

Location – Harry's Pub, Ladbroke Grove, London

Company – Solo

Time – Late Afternoon

This was a type of drinking I would now relish.
I'd become a bit of a barfly. I loved to nurse a drink with a book and while an hour or two away. It had become my thing, a way to get a rare moment to myself, sometimes an even rarer moment of reflection. More often than not it was just a way to get pissed up and let off some steam.

I never had a favourite bar or anything like that. Wherever I roamed, I would always find a place that suited my needs.

There was only one stipulation: it had to have a good vibe. Rough and tumble, upmarket or glitzy, it never mattered to me. A drink's a drink, and a place is what you make of it, that's how I looked at it all.

If I wasn't reading, I'd enjoy my hobby of talking to strangers. I specifically enjoy talking to fellow barfly characters. I'd developed an *interesting character* radar and could always sense such individuals immediately.

The class of joint never determines the quality of the character. The interesting ones transcend environment and tax brackets; they are omni-present. If the mood is right and the alcohol strong, I will end up in conversations with such folk.

That day, though, wasn't one of those days, sitting in that Ladbroke Grove watering hole I looked up from my book about jazz legend Miles Davis to see the excellent beginnings of snow starting to fall outside. It was super cold in London, and it looked like the snow was settling on the ground.

"Cool," I said out loud to no one particular.

Who doesn't like snow? It always conjures various feelings of wonderful.

I enjoyed watching it fall over the market stores and busy shoppers. I even spotted Albee my feathered friend balancing on top of a shop awning across the road. I raised my glass. I felt a bit sorry for him, it had been ages since I'd made a hint of an effort to notice his feathery presence.

I downed my drink and at the very second the glass touched table my phone started to glow and rattle with a series of incoming texts. I knew it was band-related, just a few texts from Maz. The group had a big chunk of time off because we had exhausted all the opportunities that suited our stature. We were 'cooling our heels' so to speak.

We had done everything there is to do with the album campaign. It was a 'catch lightning in a bottle' moment of success, one of which we all thought could be continued. So in a strategic bid of record label suaveness, some time away from the public eye was now in order. The idea was we could come back and do it all again. Management told me the label were planning to re-release the album as a deluxe edition with extra live versions, remixes. It sounded cool, but I didn't want to stop yet. I wasn't even a little bit ready to get off the roller coaster, but I had to admit for the betterment of the band the proposed plan made sense.

So there I was just a few days into our sabbatical when I saw the text messages land. I couldn't imagine it was anything of a pressing nature, so I carried on with my planned pit stop at Harry's worn-out bar where I would buy a local old timer a pint, and then order myself what I believed to be my third gin and tonic of the late London afternoon. G and T was my go-to drink because I was told by a model that it had the fewest calories. Info that always stuck in my mind as I was always looking for ways to stay slim.

That day in Harry's I was feeling loose, without any weighty concerns. I was even considering calling up some mates to turn the evening into a bit of a session, take it up another level, perhaps later end up in a club or whatever other madness we could find ourselves in.

That's to give you a glimpse of where my head was at.

I checked-in with my phone to see what was up with the band.

I've never ever forgotten the next few minutes.

It's funny how moments like these can be relived with such accurate detail, almost as if you can taste the moment.

It's a shame you can't pick the times that stick like this. I wish this wasn't one of them.

In a heartbeat I would swap it for any of my previous past glory moments, any of the ones that are slowly fading into the cotton candy section of my mind soon to be forgotten forever. I can still taste the low-quality gin. I can still feel the heat from the 80s style radiator. I can still see the handwritten *out of order, soz* sign on the fruit machine and I can definitely still recall the slight hint of toilet disinfectant that wafted through the pub every time someone opened the door to the bogs.

It's all in there, indelibly locked into my mind like a bad tattoo. The icy cold messages punctured in pain, each word cutting like a hot knife to the bone.

I was no longer needed in the band.

"We've concluded that as a band we need to part ways."

After ten years, I was being irrevocably discharged. Change was needed and I would not be part of the next chapter. They were calling it *creative differences*.

I looked at my phone with a wet face full of tears in the hope that what I was reading was a mistake. It was not. This was a crushing blow, sobering – as real as it gets. Instantly I had a new feeling running through my body, not that adrenaline rush type of feeling I was so used too, not the high highs of playing a sensational show or riveting performance on TV or radio. This was the opposite in every shape, way and form. I downed my drink and called the girl behind the bar to bring four more. She could see my distress and obliged without question.

Subsequently I spent the next hour on the phone trying to resolve this catastrophe, but my time had indeed come.

The cold and unforgiving sword of music business skullduggery had fallen as it so often does, only this time it was on me.

I guess devastated is the best word to describe how I felt, yet I didn't have much time to dwell on this bitter blow, as I had a previous engagement in my calendar recording drums on the new album for an up-and-coming Icelandic pop singer songwriter called Marta Rose. Marta played a black and gold sparkly guitar and had an impressive bluesy soulful voice, a cross between Janis Joplin and Freddie Mercury.

Marta specifically requested me, apparently, she liked my moves and the following day after my crushing Ladbroke Grove blow, I would be heading to Berlin for a two-month recording session, in a famous studio where apparently David Bowie and Iggy Pop once recorded.

I told no one of my heartbreaking news. I pretended like everything was alright. With hindsight I believe I was suffering from shock the whole time I was out there. I was physically in the studio, yet I certainly wasn't present. I remember very little but what I will never forget is how constantly cold I felt and how old school vintage the studio was, no internet, not a computer in sight. I remember old tape machines and rare microphones with names near impossible to pronounce. Telefunken sticks in memory.

I liked the way the word rolled out of the mouth, *Teleeey funken!*

Even though I was nearly oblivious to the making of the album. Everyone seemed happy with the results. I guess I did a decent job.

It was the session in Germany's icy cold Berlin surrounded by vintage Telefunkens, after Ladbroke Grove's devastation, that perhaps temporarily saved me. I wasn't out of the woods yet, not even close.

Once I returned to London, Libby rather dubiously asked me to meet her at the little cafe by the lake in Regent's Park. I noticed Albee was there enjoying a nub of a croissant, he looked up to me and nodded, I nodded back. Old mates.

Libby was already waiting for me, no hugs or smiles were offered, instead it was straight to the business of dumping my ass – perhaps even a world record – fifteen seconds into sitting down and the deed was done. She was out the door leaving only a faint smell of Diptyque perfume mixing with the freshly fried full English breakfast being delivered to the man in paint splattered overalls sitting at the next table.

I waited for the final waft of her fancy French scent to be overwhelmed by the various cafe aromas before I got up to pay for her cappuccino and blueberry muffin. I then went about finding the nearest pub. I found many ultimately ending up at The Betsy Trotwood in Farringdon. This public house was my new sanctuary, a place where my only goal was to get completely out of my mind drunk, it was a simple but highly effective task.

Emotionally I had bitten far more off than I could chew, and I found comfort eating and getting completely blitzed out of my mind to be a much better solution than dealing with my new reality.

After getting fucked up, I would order takeaway after takeaway, five or six in a row, completely unaware of what I ordered, most of the time forgetting and being woken up by baguette-handed George the concierge at my door carrying bags of the stuff. I would drink, drug then gorge myself into gluttonous stupor. More often or not I would then throw it all up, and like Groundhog Day, the next day I would do exactly the same again.

The band was gone, and Libby had bailed. The latter wasn't really a big shock, since without the band I was just an everyday bloke. That's simply not what ladies like Libby want.

Being extra honest, I really hadn't been the greatest of boyfriends. The typical issues really. Bad at communication, inconsiderate, infidelity?

Whilst we were an item I certainly flirted past a few bases with a female companion or two and I absolutely definitely missed, not one, but two of her birthdays during our tenure.

Sadly, I could go on.

If I told you I was trying to change my behaviour, you wouldn't believe me, but the thing is I really was.

This emotional upset in the grand scheme of my current predicaments was small fry as I was absolutely inconsolable with the loss of the band. I was heartbroken, thoroughly depressed, my pride was crushed, and I felt completely humiliated, mortified, worthless. I could go on and on.

The time that followed dragged by. It could have been months or years for all I knew or cared. I dropped off the map bar checking in occasionally with my family, always by phone, on which I found it far easier to put on an act.

I spared everyone my sadness – much simpler than having to worry about the fam worrying about me. I didn't need that extra sauce. One afternoon during this hazy limbo I was half watching day-time television when a stylish advert aimed at recruiting folk for the army appeared on my TV. What I saw seemed like a pretty sweet deal and a quick search online took me to their website where I began to fill out a series of forms. I was a lost boy at this juncture and really that's a complete understatement. I had spent almost a decade pursuing the dream of making the band famous. I had given my heart and soul to the process.

What was left to do?

What was left to give?

I now felt like I had nothing left to offer other than serve for the royal armed forces, feel some of that camaraderie they advertised with such emphasis on TV. I was convinced this was my best and only option to go forwards.

Disappointment really does have a habit of inciting extreme change, doesn't it?

While you're in the middle of such a moment most things seem very bleak indeed, even my taste buds couldn't handle the beating my broken heart had received, as all the flavours I once sought out with total adventurous glee now felt dull and listless. Perhaps the only positive outcome to my turmoil was that I would lose loads of weight, yet even that made me feel sick. A trip to my doctor and series of tests revealed that I was severely malnourished, massively dehydrated and completely deficient in all vitamins and minerals that contribute to feeling good in your own skin.

This was not adding anything positive to my already dire situation, and to be frank, if there was anyone who would be less cut out for a role in the army it would be me.

What was I thinking, eh?

I guess I wasn't. Just reacting in an extreme manner to my devastating predicament. I can't even tolerate a needle injection or blood in a movie. I'm not afraid of hard work though.

In hindsight perhaps I could have used my intense work ethic to make my way up through the ranks.

General Morrison!

Captain Pop!

Has a ring to it doesn't it?

As I was tapping away at the computer the elevator intercom buzzer rang. It was Nancy who wanted to come up to collect the rest of Libby's belongings.

"Come right up Nance, all good."

When Nancy arrived, she noticed my furrowed look of grit and determination as I hunched over the laptop, all squinty eyed and ham handed.

"What you up too, Pop?"

"I'm joining the army, Nance."

"Oh no you're not," she promptly responded, setting me straight by pushing the laptop screen closed and announcing:

"We're going out!"

Our destination, the cinema.

Nancy felt sorry for me. Libby had moved on quickly. She was now dating a singer in a band with way more hits and far more fans than I ever had.

It stung, but it was nothing in comparison to the dagger wounds inflicted by losing the band. There was no ill will with Libby – that was placed elsewhere. Nancy drove me to the theatre in her tiny green Mini Cooper and we listened to classical music without a word being spoken the whole way there. It wasn't an uncomfortable silence, just an appreciation for the music I guess. I noticed cigarette buts in the ash tray, I remember she was trying to quit.

Why say anything?

Quitting is hard.

I have no recollection of the film other than there was a dragon and a tiger involved.

After the flick Nancy dropped me home. It was just before midnight and the evening was hot and humid. Thanks to Nancy there would be no joining the army, instead I roamed the sweaty streets of London. At some point I found myself crossing Westminster bridge. I could see the warmly illuminated Big Ben clock. It was just before midnight. As I crossed the Thames, I looked at the fast-flowing river below and thought about throwing myself in. Instead, I took my gloom-riddled spontaneity as an opportunity to throw my phone into the murky water instead. "FUCK IT," I shouted in disdain as it left my clammy hand to a destination of doom. I didn't need it, no one needed me, and I needed no one. "FUCK IT!"

The walk continued until I found an offy where I bought myself a 25-year-old scotch and a packet of Viennese whirl biscuits, both of which I would attempt to consume all by myself. I finished the biscuits, and with a jumper full of sweet buttery crumbs the scotch did the desired job of taking me to my own private hideaway – an unconscious oblivion located a few doors down from heartbreak hotel and the misery street cafe.

Booze and drugs were like the training wheels on a kid's bike, keeping me semi balanced and active, yet they were also stopping me from falling down completely.

The trouble is, as I would later learn, the hitting the ground part is a key ingredient in getting yourself back up.

I wasn't allowing that moment to happen. I was in denial: one of the worst, bitterest stages of grieving.

I can't deny I didn't *not* think about ending it all, jumping off one of London's bridges or something equally life-ending like that. I thought about my old phone hitting the water and beginning its smooth descent to the bottom. I imagined it was me sinking slowly, watching the light from the street lamps getting duller and duller the closer I got to the river bed. This is when something disturbing happened. Everything went pitch black and I was unable to move except for an inch here or there. I realised I was somehow in a wooden box, a coffin. Instinctively I knew I was at the bottom of the Thames.

When I worked out where I was and what was happening, I tried to push or wiggle to some sort of freedom before quickly realising that I was utterly stuck. This is when my breathing became fast, the hotness of my breath condensing on my skin from the boxy casket lid hovering a mere millimetre from my face. I began to panic with every cell of my body wanting to escape. I shouted and screamed but there's only deathly silence, bar of course the familiar ringing in my ears. My heart's pumping to the point of bursting in a tremendous stress-induced feeling of lonesome hopelessness until the whole claustrophobic experience ended with me somehow lying in bed completely shaken to the core covered in sweat. This was my first ever panic attack.

In slow motion I flicked the bedside lamp on and, without looking, began to feel around on the cold marble floor where I knew I'd purposely left a half-finished can of extra strong lager or something savage like that from one of the nights before. I took a couple of decent swigs from the flat vile tasting brew and lit a cigarette. I took a few drags before croaking,

"WHAT THE FUCK WAS THAT?"

I tried to write down the experience into a makeshift diary, basically the back of an envelope, probs a bill. It wasn't happening, I couldn't be bothered, I got a few words in.

(Diary extract)

I think I had my first panic attack!

As I sat in bed, puffing away, I began to cry. I was so tired, not sleepy tired, but emotionally tired. I was mentally shattered, utterly exhausted, I remember feeling like I couldn't be bothered with anything anymore.

A few weeks passed. I can't recall the day or month. What I do remember is being woken up to the tedious rhythmic vibrations of my mobile phone buried somewhere in the depths of my trouser pocket laying amongst a heap of dirty clothing in the middle of the room.

I was begrudgingly awake with no plans other than to turn the blower off and go back to sleep. Of course I had no real reason to be up yet.

Completely starkers and totally befuddled, I got out of bed on a mission to locate the offending phone. As I pulled it from my vintage, slightly bobbled pin stripe slacks I was surprised to see an unusually high number of missed calls and text messages, which was weird considering how few people had my new number, especially since my old number was now somewhere at the bottom of the river Thames.

The attitude at this point was very much, fuck my life, fuck the band, fuck it all.

As I tapped the covert four-digit security code (1,2,3,4) into the cheap dog and bone contraption, my intention had changed from wanting to silence the device, to see who's curiously blowing it up. The second before this information was revealed the battery died and the shiny block of plastic in my hand descended into darkness.

For a moment or two I thought about plugging the phone in to charge, but I was now wide awake and decided I had a much better plan of action to instigate.

The pursuit?

A blowout binge of the absolute obliteration variety.

If there was a meter that measured binges my upcoming endeavour would set the needle all the way to top – a binge of epic proportions, the no holds barred from here to infinity type of drinking bender.

With only my obliviotic thoughts running through my head I was dressed and ready to go, wallet in pocket and the key to my crib on a thick silver chain hanging around my neck, where it couldn't easily be lost.

I lit my last smoke and headed off into the late London afternoon to see what type of distraction I could get myself into. I stuck to my plan with vigour and the subsequent hours and days become a blur, perhaps beyond a blur and more of a mirage. I was blackout drunk and high on God knows what. When I finally emerged, I was in a complete state. I snuck out of whoever's bed I was sharing completely battered and bruised.

I decided I needed a short 'time out' before getting back into my important mission. After all it wouldn't complete itself, the art of keeping totally inebriated requires much effort and diligence. I took this work very seriously.

It was early in the morning and London's nine to five work force was heading out to their day of hard graft and soft procrastination. When I caught sight of my dishevelled reflection in the glass facade of my building it made me feel, well, even sadder than I already was. I barely recognised myself. I looked like I had been throwing myself around one of those TV advert army obstacle courses that I almost signed up for. It looked like I'd been crawling under barbed wire or climbing over flaming tanks or other such extremes.

I don't know what the hell I had been up to.

I didn't want to know. I didn't care.

What was my new catch phrase again? Ah yeah, Fuck it!

My only plan of action was to hit the rain box immediately and drink a pint of cold orange juice before getting right back out on the drunkard's horse. Time was of the essence as I had to do all of this before the effects of the previous night's intoxicants began to clear and I started to feel again. I had reason. I was extra disappointed in myself. It transpired that all those missed calls were from my Mum. I had forgotten Grandma's birthday! I was now drinking to forget and it was working. Before I knew it I was back out having an uneventful day continuing to drown my sorrows whilst taking on the noble task of propping up the bar at the 'The Lord Nelson' or 'The Governor' or whatever it was called. I stayed there until closing time. I even bought myself a cheeky bottle of red to sip on during the walk back to my gaff. A drink of this nature is called a *traveller*.

At this point in my life, journeys from watering holes, especially after closing time always fare better with a *traveller*.

That night I got back well, and the next morning I woke up from the longest sleep I'd had in years.

You know what?

I'd completely forgotten what a good night's sleep felt like and as I slowly regained memory of the previous day's events. I remembered exactly what had enabled this outstanding rest.

At some point after getting back from the boozer I found a small bag of magic mushrooms in a Barbour jacket I once wore to Glastonbury festival. This jacket was in the back of my wardrobe and for some reason caught my eye when I drunkenly started to try do laundry at 2.30 in the morning. I began with the right intention yet with my traveller still in hand I came to a 'better', or should I say, 'easier' solution of just throwing all my dirty clothing into one focused pile behind a sliding door in the master bedroom aka the wardrobe. The shrooms I discovered looked like dried raisins and I assumed all potency from them was gone, regardless I threw them into an oversized Mickey Mouse mug with some hot water and a shot of Tequila and guzzled it all down like a hungry cat with a bowl of fresh cream.

For a moment I thought I was correct with my potency assumptions.

I wasn't.

Not long after consuming the fungal brew I was out like a light, completely gone, SAYONARA.

There were no swirls, twirls, morphing or melting, no hallucinations or cosmic visions, nothing of the kind, it was just me knocked out cold, dead to the world.

When groggy Pop woke up next day and staggered over to the bathroom, I saw something that damn near gave me a heart attack, it was a quick pre wiz glance in the mirror that stopped me dead in my tracks.

I couldn't believe my eyes. They had to be playing tricks!

I hurriedly rubbed my sleepy peepers then splashed cold water on my face and hesitantly looked again.

"Oh man."

Something was very wrong.

I threw some more water on my face and opened the blinds, letting the day's unobstructed sunlight fill the bathroom. It must be a trick of the light or something like that.

I rushed to my mobile phone which was in the bedroom and quickly took a selfie.

"Nah, this ain't happening man," I said in response to the photograph.

I headed back to the bathroom where I turned on the rain box and just stood there in my boxer shorts and Thin Lizzy tee until I felt completely sopping stupid.

Leaving a tsunami Morrison-like trail of water behind me I went straight to the massive mirror by my private lift.

When me and that mirror reacquainted ourselves, I needed no more proof.

The moment I saw my reflection I let out a huge scream.

"FUUUUUCK."

I still considered myself a young man but what was looking back at me in the mirror was a shock to say the least.

My hair had gone grey!

Not just a few hairs here and there.

NOPE!

My whole curly haired medusa like Barnet was now a silvery old geezer colour. Overnight my once dark hazelnut shade had turned grey on me. What the hell was going on?

I then remembered that mug of mushroom tea I drank the night before and somehow instantly assumed this was a side effect.

What to do?

I got myself a stiff Jack Daniels and completely freaked out. At the peak of my mania, I called the doctor who rang me back a few hours later. I was in a completely different mood by then as I was three quarters of the way through the bottle and drunk enough to be calling Jack, Dave. Dave Daniels really is a horrible drink, but at the time it was nearest to hand. I once had boxes of the stuff. I returned home from tour years ago and they were all there neatly stacked in the larder. I never questioned it.

"Cool."

When I told Doctor Grace that I'd drunk a five-year-old magic mushroom tea procured from Glastonbury festival and now all my hair had gone grey, she laughed.

Doctor Grace looked after lots of artists. She was a touring doctor. I think she travelled with bands like Mötley Crüe and Aerosmith. She was a therapist, acupuncturist, masseuse, nutritionist and most importantly chemist. She had the golden ticket, the ability to prescribe drugs. Dr Grace didn't realise it at first, but the latter was always the real reason any band would shell out the amount of money it costs to travel with a 'rock doctor'.

Dr Grace knew all about my topsy turvy life. Her prognosis: STRESS!

She said, "it either falls out, goes grey, or both."

I would much rather have grey hair than no hair, so I thanked her and hung up. I then put Pink Floyd's *Dark Side of the Moon* on really loud and drank the rest of my Jill Daniels.

Year – 2004

Location – London

Mood – Reckless

My biggest issue? The part I just couldn't get over? I missed the band. I missed absolutely everything about it. I was hardwired to perform. Promo had been programmed into my very existence. How about this for a cruel joke? At 8.30 every night I would still get that pre-show excitement rush followed closely by the tingling sensation of butterflies in my belly. Yes, it's any performer's nemesis, the pre-show nerves, the calm before the storm. It was now only a phantom feeling as I had no stage or band to play with. I'd gone onstage at exactly 8.45 every night for so many years. I'd got so used to that intense pre-adrenalin, pre-endorphin kick that when I didn't get that once so familiar rush, the phantom feeling replaced it.

I was in show business, yet I had no business to show.

This phantom feeling went on for years. Every time 8.30 rolled around, I would be hit with a cruel hormonal hailstorm of memories of my old life. It was specifically about the music, the live performances, the shows, gosh, THE SHOWS. What wouldn't I to do be there again?

I always loved starting the first song of our concerts with this simple drumbeat:

Dum, ba, dum dum, ba, dum, ba, dum dum, ba,

It's a variation on the most famous drum beat ever: *We will rock you*' by Queen which goes like this:

Dum dum ba, dum dum ba, dum dum ba, dum dum ba.

Now I know 'dum' and 'ba' are not official musical notations, but it works rather well at illustrating my point.

I will never forget this *start of the show* moment on my red acrylic drum set. Although I can recall all the beautiful drum sets I acquired over the years and easily match them with this bittersweet reminiscence, I just can't help loving my acrylic kit a little extra. For one, it was see-through, or *rose tinted* and because of this transparency we could set up lights inside all the drums. Say no more, right? It was the most attention-grabbing kit I had.

So as that first hit of adrenalin rushed through me, I would begin my beat. Always mid-tempo, cool as a cucumber. There really is nothing worse than a drummer in a rush, is there?

I would ride that rhythm until it started cooking in the room. Only when I could feel the audience simmering would I start a long-drawn-out snare drum roll, getting faster and faster and louder and louder, until I would suddenly stop, like I'd been frozen in ice. After the drumming frenzy I'd stirred up this would always, without fail, create a fever pitch frenzy in the room. After my lengthy pause I would hit the crash cymbal introducing Vic and his wailing Marshall amplified Fender Stratocaster guitar licks. Vic was a virtuoso, doing the work of two musicians. He was also a whiz with electronics. He'd cleverly wired his guitar not only to his classic Marshall stack amplifier, but his hysterically acquired fender bass man amp.

"It's the King Kong of bass amps," said Deptford Dan the vendor of such a bottom end monster.

"How much you want for it?" Vic asked.

"Four Monkeys for you mate!" Deptford responded, continuing his primate theme.

Four monkeys was two thousand pounds well spent because Vic's additional low end rumble was tremendous, just like King Kong.

Our guitar maestro's hands were massive too, Vic's long fingers could reach to play the high notes on the thinnest strings of his guitar, precisely following the vocal melody whilst at the same time plucking the bass notes in metronomic time with me, the beat keeper, the engine of the ship.

COLOSSAL is the word. King Kong who?

Once Vic had his moment, Maz would then magically appear, often in an intentional cloud of smoke and the room would erupt like a volcano of good energy. The sight set off another kick, adrenalin rush number two.

Wooooosh.

We were off.

Typically, songs flew by in this state.

It wasn't a "going through the motions" situation, quite the opposite. More akin to a surfer riding the wave, you're going with it, highly alert yet in a perfect flow, all the practice and hard work paying off in an act of excellent execution. This feeling was sheer and utter bliss, a feeling preserved only in experience.

Experience is what led us to build moments into our songs where we'd purposely go off-piste, allowing the unexpected to occur, admitting a spotlight for mayhem and misadventure.

The end results were equally blissful and often more physical than musical. I recall a gig in Stockholm where we led the entire audience out of the venue around the city central square and back into the club, the whole time in an all singing, all dancing conga line. Guitar solos, drum solos, a cappella vocal solos. We took our moments and ran with them, something which only made our shows more impressive. We couldn't have done any of this without the band's lead singer.

Without our fearless front-person, we wouldn't have had the musical scope to get where we were going to on stage, crossing genres from rock to jazz through to soul, back to blues where we could, if we wanted, take a night cap in reggae, folk or samba. It might look easy written down like this, but really it's not light musical work, aside from our supreme ability to play our instruments and our natural musical synergy. I believe it was Maz and her special voice that was the glue that bound this sonic tomfoolery together. I missed that voice bad.

These hail stone memories brought up another long-forgotten gem of a memory – playing a theatre in Rotterdam where everything that could possibly break, broke. My kick pedal shattered, the drum skins ripped, cymbal stands fell over, guitar amps blew up. It was a cacophony of unfortunate events, yet despite it all we still kept it together. We used all we had left, our voices, going full on a cappella on the audience. We did what we did best and got the crowd involved, we stood at the lip of the stage and sang with all the power we could possibly muster. I'm getting goosebumps now thinking of it: memories of a Wonderboy!

It wasn't the performance the audience expected that night, yet it was the most rock and roll experience they would ever get. I guess that sums it up really. My old life wasn't typical; it was extraordinary, and boy did I miss it! Without the band I lacked purpose and direction, I felt anonymous.

It's around this time I stopped going back to Pop's Penthouse. It didn't feel like a home anymore. If I had to go back I would just look around in disgust, the sheer arrogance of it all now felt completely inappropriate.

"A rock star would live here," I said out loud whilst skulking around looking for a reason why I belonged there. "Shame I'm not one anymore," I muttered, even hearing my own voice saying it stung. It wasn't Pop's Palace anymore.

I didn't belong there; it almost felt like I was trespassing.

A few days later, the trespasser was heading out to meet my dealer at the greasy spoon around the corner. I stepped out of the elevator onto the ground floor where Big George was sitting at the concierge desk. He handed me a red envelope.

I stepped outside into a fresh, crisp autumn afternoon and carelessly opened the envelope ripping the pink card inside.

It was an invitation. A mistake I'm sure, but that didn't matter to me one bit. I had been invited to a swanky new club opening in Knightsbridge, free drinks. SOLD. 'Amore Amore' here I come.

Once again, I have no memory of the time that passed after that night, no idea of how many days or weeks had gone by – very much how it was going for me in the time department, a reoccurring theme and a most notable byproduct of being black out drunk.

I only have two real memories from this time. One was the devastating news that Swiss army Eddie had died. I don't recall how I found out, but I called Radish his ex-boyfriend, I knew they hadn't been an item for a while, but there was no way he wouldn't have had the lowdown on Eddie's demise. Turns out he was on tour with some glam metal band, he missed a lobby call and after endless buzzes and knocking on his door, hotel security eventually discovered dear Eddie dead in his bed. The autopsy revealed he hit his head sometime after the band's show. He'd gone to bed after eating a four-cheese pizza and never woke up. I was going to go to his funeral, but I am ashamed to admit I slept through it.

That's a lie!

I woke up, acknowledged the time, something I had absolutely plenty of, more than enough to make my way across the city to his wake, but I couldn't bear to see anyone from my past. Instead, I chugged shamefully on something strong until I passed out. It was all too clear that running away is a solo race, one I was trying extremely hard to win.

I felt truly terrible when I woke up – hollow – the whole episode sent me on a spiral slow dive. I was properly on one.

My next tangible memory is where we began this story, waking up on a cold, hard, unforgiving floor.

As I started to get used to not being unconscious anymore, I scanned the darkened room. I could see sink, pots, pans, a stove. I was lying on someone's kitchen floor, one I didn't recognize. I began to coax myself up when I soon discovered I was surrounded by smashed wine bottles and cockney claret.

An excruciating pain rushed from my left hand, and on further examination I was greeted with a nasty cut. That explained the blood, the events leading up to the gash were still a mystery, although I imagined the broken wine bottles were the culprits.

I picked myself up with no idea what had happened, where I was or where I had been.

Like I said, if you drink more than your body can handle your mind will check out. It's a survival instinct. I can't stress enough, the type of drinking I was indulging in could be classed as a combat sport. My mind simply couldn't bear witness to the abuse any longer, so it let me get on with it while it hid somewhere else.

Soon enough a bleached blonde rocker in his mid-20s entered the room. He was called Sparky.

I didn't know Sparky, but I knew his footsteps.

I'd heard them stomping about above me as I lay conked out on the floor. The noise probably woke me up. I got up the moment they got louder and louder until the door swung open and, "Hey Pop, it's Sparky!" entered the room and my day began.

Sparky was wearing only boxer shorts and gleaming white sports socks with Adidas sliders. He energetically navigated himself around the broken glass and opened the tie-dyed curtains allowing sunlight to fill my eyes in the most unwelcome fashion. Shortly after this blinding entrance Sparky handed me a hot drink – it was either weak tea or weaker coffee, it didn't matter.

"The world's cold brother, so you better start the day with a hot drink," said Sparky.

I took a proper look at my host's eyes which looked like tiny black grapes set in his gaunt pale face.

There was no mistaking it, young Sparky was still tripping balls, which is probably why the gruesome sight of blood and broken glass didn't seem to bother him. I couldn't help pigeonholing this fella, but to me he looked like the reckless member of a boy band, or some new emerging model signed to an agency with a name like '*prestige*' or '*pristine*.'

I welcomed the beverage with my undamaged hand and wondered what drugs Sparky was on. I hoped I'd been taking the same.

Whilst I inspected my damaged hand under the bright glow of daylight Sparky wisely stated,

"You should get that checked out, dude."

"I think I probably should," I responded.

My surprising nonchalance indicated to me that I had indeed been taking the same medicine as Sparky.

As Sparky got himself comfortable on a seen-better-days sofa covered in various moth riddled throws and mis-matching pillows at the far end of the kitchen slash living room he rolled a joint which in truth was the only reason I hadn't got the hell out of dodge just yet. The rationale being I hoped the weed would take the edge off how horrendous I felt. As 'Sparky' was preparing the biffta he waffled on endlessly about the night we'd apparently had. I really had no interest. I couldn't keep up with his hyper pace, instead I tuned him out and stared at my hot drink. I imagined the frothy bubbles subtly moving and morphing into shapes within the chipped mug to be like wispy cumulus clouds blowing their way through a mahogany caffeinated sky.

I thought about how nice it would be to be that frothy warm cloud in Sparky's chipped mug. Instead, I was perching uncomfortably on a rickety old wooden stool focusing on the gentle piano music playing through a radio somewhere in the kitchen. I guess I'd been conscious enough to remember that I had one other clear memory – a dream from the night before.

All these thoughts were put on pause when it became very clear I had an immediate date with a hospital. A few hours later I was giving my name, age and birthplace to a cordial lady at hospital admittance.

I was visiting these medical establishments a lot at this time. I had developed a great talent in catching 'DRI's' (Drink Related Injuries.)

I made a point of not visiting the same hospital each time. Let's just say London has a lot of hospitals.

My previous visit was the result of me falling down an escalator in Kings Cross station utterly intoxicated on Absinthe – a drink that is illegal in many countries. I hit the dirty station floor with a bang, the thud reverberated and echoed in the cavernous space, which accompanied an awful bloody split to the back of my head.

It happened to be the very same spot on my head I split open as a young Wonderboy, when I fell out of my grandparent's apple tree whilst exploring its gnarly upper branches.

Back then the doctor used super glue to fix me, this time round three staples. If it ever happens again, I can't imagine what other type of arts and crafts products they would use to mend me, Sellotape, blue tac, perhaps even elastic bands.

So, there I was at the hospital with my new DRI – a sliced up sore swollen bloody hand. I knew the drill and after signing in I visited a row of vending machines in the main foyer. I had exactly one pound fifty, enough for a drink and two mildly great snacks, or one drink and one great snack (Dr Pepper and a chunky flapjack). As I sat waiting to be seen by a doctor of any description, my weed high finally dissipated and I was left feeling a five-letter word I tried to avoid at all costs, S O B E R.

Trying to take my mind off that horrible five-letter word, I munched away on my sweet treat whilst watching all the poor fuckers who were temporarily, or perhaps permanently, calling this place home.

I nodded in and out of this reflective state for most of the day. The whole time thinking 'I must do everything I can to never come back here again'. I thought these thoughts until I was taken into a brightly lit room tucked away behind a big blue curtain, where I sat alone until a young doctor came to inspect my wound and stitch me up.

"What's your profession, Mr Morrison?" she asked.

"I'm a drummer."

"Well, Mr Morrison any deeper and you could have lost some serious mobility in this hand. You're very lucky indeed, you won't be able to play drums for at least a month or until the stitches fall out."

'LUCKY!'

I hadn't felt lucky in quite some time.

She was right though.

To lose the ability to play my beloved drums would have been the last straw.

The doctor's words rattled round my mind. I was convinced I had turned a corner and I vowed for the first time ever to clean up my act.

This lasted until I got back to Pop's stupid palace, and I called my extortionate lawyer, who, along with my accountant, I had been purposely ignoring for months.

For some reason the remaining band members were dragging their feet with the legal and financial aspects of me not being in the group any longer.

"Think of it like a divorce," the lawyer said.

He told me that the band had already got a new drummer and apparently, they were making a new album. He thought the plan to eject me from the group had been in play for quite some time. "That extended break brought on by your label was a rather large fib, a Trojan horse to help them achieve what they really wanted. You were last to know Pop, but because of this you should receive a far healthier settlement deal."

"This makes me feel even fucking worse," I shouted spicily.

"One more thing Pop, your accountant has an urgent message for me to relay to you. You have limited to zero funds. They feel you can find better counsel elsewhere." Translation: you're broke, and we want nothing to do with you!

Things were getting messy.

Conversations like this required a stiff drink, so with my newly acquired stitches and throbbing hand I headed to the fridge aka 'the budget bar' where I thought FUCK IT and poured myself a full pint of cheap white wine.

I downed half the vinegary liquid with a grimace and only then did I finally commit to writing down the most important part of the bloody day, you see as I lay unconscious on Sparky's kitchen floor I had been back to room 613 at the Gershwin hotel and relived the moment I discovered Drewford Alabama's book. This came with another cryptic message that I wrote down with a silver sharpie onto a Chinese takeaway menu.

Jamie Morrison

TIME IS ON YOUR SIDE

and

A
V

The year – 2006

Mood – Phased and Confused

Location – Lost

I guess I'd been 'cavalier' with my finances.
My ignorance had been bliss and the price tag far greater than I ever anticipated. All my monetary needs were wrapped up with the band and life on the road or in the studio, I had many financial plans beyond my extravagant spending habits, but none of them involved me not being in the group. There was no safety net for that scenario. Why would there be?

I had navigated myself into an awful situation every way I turned.

I could have asked my folks, perhaps even my Grandparents for help, but I was too proud, and in truth, too embarrassed to ask.

Sitting here today, I don't believe that there's anything noble in not asking for help.

Back then I was lost and confused, asking for help seemed to be a further admission of failure. I was balancing perilously close to an irrational emotional precipice, nothing made sense.

In what felt like overnight my flashy possessions were sold off to pay my legal bills and day to day living.

I moved from my swanky 'rock star' penthouse apartment, which I now fully resented, into a tiny room inside a tinier house shared with five law students on a road behind Kings Cross station that you wouldn't want to be caught alone on at nighttime.

That's the warning my new house mates gave me anyway.

I didn't care. I wouldn't be paying any attention to their advice.

I thought whatever happened on those streets after dark may be a welcome way to escape the mess I was in. I was aware that doing yourself in only ever moves the pain to others, but being done over by the hands of another?

Sure, why not.

"Try me!" I imagined I would shout to anyone lurking in those darkened alleyways and shadowed streets. "What do I care?"

Regardless of downsizing, I got on well with my new housemates and found it a not so bad scene at all. It was suitably fitting for my new position in life. I found it oddly refreshing to live in shared accommodation again, although these kids lived like adults, whereas at Benjy's we lived like students.

One day I heard about some auditions happening across town for a soul singer with a bunch of Grammies. It would be a year's worth of very well-paid work. Naturally I signed myself up for a try-out, the major issue standing in my way was funds. I was so broke I couldn't afford the train fare to get me across town to the Hammersmith Apollo for the auditions.

I borrowed some money from one of my new house mates and with the necessary shekels rattling around in my pocket I set off one early morning to see if I could get a job with the only real tangible skill I had – drumming.

Auditioning was oddly nerve racking, best described as swan like – I looked graceful above water but below, behind the scenes so to speak I was kicking wildly just trying to keep afloat. Considering I hadn't picked up a pair of sticks in nearly eighteen months my playing was decent, I was certainly not as sharp as I once was, but I thought I did good. With hindsight that was probably down to the Dutch courage I had before leaving the house because I couldn't have been more wrong with my 'I did good' rhythmic assessment.

The musical director called me later, while I was right in the middle of doing some washing. You see, in return for borrowing my train fare to Hammersmith, I said I would do my flatmate's laundry. I was literally folding another bloke's Calvin Kleins when the call came in. It was pants! The 'MD' said I wasn't the right guy for the job. I had to ask, I wish I hadn't but it turns out I wasn't even in the artists' top three favourites. I let the sobering news sink in. As I did, there was a rustling at the window. I looked up, it was Albee. "Fucking Albee!" I was being harsh. It wasn't Albee's fault, this was my own. Realising this I went back to folding undies, as I did it dawned on me that I was now a three-word phrase I didn't feel fantastic about, and no, it's not fluff and fold.

Broke unemployed musician.

I needed a job. Any job.

Later, with the rest of my well-earned laundry money, I went on a rampage of bar hopping. I was extra amped as my ego had been freshly bruised by not securing that job I desperately needed.

"You're a complete loser," was the constant looping mantra running through my head.

As per I was solo when I hit an all glass mirrored, black and gold affair of a late-night drinking establishment somewhere in Marylebone. It must have been a full moon for I was being fully belligerent, throwing drinks, swearing, general drunken obnoxiousness, I was being a right pain in the ass, to such an extent that the clubs rather large security team decided I deserved a tune up, a shoeing, a kick in. I had pissed off some serious folk and subsequently was forcefully taken into a back-room office where I was slapped in the face by a bear of a man and told explicitly to sit down and not move. The slap was an appetiser for the beating of my life which was well on its way – at least that's how my intoxicated mind could see it play out.

In anticipation of my impending thrashing, I popped two pills I had from a few nights earlier, molly apparently. I figured it would help ease my way through the next hour. So there I was, braced for a beating with the muffled din of Guns and Roses 'Welcome to the Jungle' seeping through the walls from the dance floor when a smartly dressed, very attractive older woman arrived with a pack of juiced up security all with neck tattoos and buzz cuts. The lady sat at the desk opposite me and placed a black cigarette procured from a silver box between her rouge lips. As she did one of the security men walked over and fired up a lighter. I watched the lady watch me whilst she took a few elegant drags, exhaling the smoke so it travelled in my direction clouding her face.

"What's your name?" Her smooth words mixing with the tobacco in the air.

"I am Pop. Pop Fucking Morrison," I said full of piss and vinegar… I matched none of the intrigue or suave the lady was using. Booze really does make you stupid, doesn't it?

What happened next was surprising to say the least.

"Wait you're POP MORRISON?"

"Yeah!" I grunted like a pig.

"The drummer?"

Now even in my wildly intoxicated state I could still appreciate that what was going on wasn't normal. At this point the lady expertly switched up her upper-class English twang to speak in an eastern European accent to the bulky men in the room behind me,

"I don't make the habit of remembering musicians' names, but my son was infatuated with you. He's a drummer and one Christmas years back he met you with his father after one of your performances. You signed a pair of your drumsticks for him. Pop Morrison, let me just say my boy Caleb practiced relentlessly with those signed sticks. So much so your signature wore away. It's quite a thing that our paths have crossed tonight. I just got word that Caleb got the job offer from an audition he did earlier today. My boy has gone pro and is off on tour for a year's worth of very well-paid work with a female artist who recently won a Grammy or two. I am so proud! Enough about me, can I do anything for you? I would like to help. If there's anything you need, I am obliged to try get it for you, you inspired my son, and for that I am eternally grateful."

My head was now cooked with the pills taking full effect, the room was spinning, and I could feel myself drifting off to some other dimension. As best as I possibly could, I announced that I needed a job and a bed, I then in slow motion collapsed into a heap.

It didn't end there as I still have a clear memory of another conversation, only this one I do believe continued as I was unconscious, I guess it was just a pissed-up, passed-out dream.

The first clue that it was dreamlike was that I was eloquent and articulate. The reality was that before I passed out, I could barely see, let alone speak. In my unconscious oblivion I tell the elegant club maître d', Caleb's mother how my drumming wasn't optimal in the audition, but I am very glad indeed that Caleb got the job.

"It feels like a win for me too, like my influence big or small has perhaps helped contribute to inspiring the next generation of drummers. As much as I needed that gig, I understand why it wasn't for me," I smiled as I drifted off to deeper more inebriated place.

The next day I woke up extremely hungover. As I gathered myself, I saw a note on the bedside table.

Call this number if you want a job.

I guessed it was from my benefactor, the elegant lady from last night, Caleb's Mum, pro-touring drummer.

I sobered up a little and called the number. Subsequently I got a gig working the VIP guest list at the door of a club in Soho called OAK. I was that person with a clipboard sandwiched between two security guards. My job was to make sure any celebs or high-spending customers got into the building without having to queue with the normal folk. I hated it but I had no choice. I had the steady job I needed to pay my steady bills. It wasn't all misery business: I appreciated that I worked at night, and that I was supplied with booze and whatever unmentionables were knocking about.

After work I would party with whoever was around at one of the many seedy after hours drinking establishments I was now privy to. That was my routine until it was time to skulk back home to sleep the upcoming day away. I did that for six days a week for a year and half before I started to forget that I was once a drummer, a drummer in a band, to fit this theme I instinctively dulled down my vibrant wardrobe, stayed clean shaven and cut my big grey curly hair military grade short. I was going for the exact opposite of what I had before I was unrecognisable.

I lost my outlandish panache and gained a more conservative look appropriate for my job as a clipboard checker.

I had two suits which I alternated throughout the week. These suits had none of the zest or vintage flair for which I was once known for. My new wardrobe incited a few mildly offensive comments like, "Hey Pop, you an estate agent now or what?"

"Sure, why not?" I would say, dead pan. Daggered words or laced questions were never my thing, those who use them even less so.

Who was I kidding? None of my old clothes fitted me anymore. It had been three years since I was fired from the band, and I had abused myself for all of it. I was the biggest I had ever been. I had let myself go in the weight department. I had let myself go in *all* departments.

My eating had got so bad some of my favourite take-away restaurants started to limit my weekly orders. There's only so many portions of pad thai you can order before someone starts questioning the health of the consumer on the receiving end of the delivery. When I moved out of Casa Del Pop the vast quantity of fast-food trash was an embarrassment. In fact, I was fined three grand which I didn't have! This ended me up in court which increased the sum to six grand. I ended up on a deal where I pay a tenner a week. Pathetic.

It was during this dress down time of my life I started carrying around a thick brown vintage briefcase with shiny silver trim. I liked the idea of it. I saw it on eBay and couldn't resist. I was going to 'work' everyday, a briefcase is what a person who works must have.

My contents were very different. For starters I had a Sega 'game gear.'

Do you recall these vintage computer games?

I always wanted one and after paying off a debt or two I treated myself. I had all the popular games: Road Rash, Sonic the Hedgehog, Mortal Kombat! My briefcase also had a very cool James Bond feature in the form of a false bottom. The clasps that closed and locked the case were unique and rotated on a 360-degree angle with a very smooth and satisfying action. If you turned the clasps 90 degrees when the case was fully open it would unlock the secret compartment at the base.

It was a class act, my briefcase. I certainly loved the way it made me feel when I carried it around.

My new life was not all bad, and after about eight or nine months, I enjoyed a little job satisfaction. I was grateful to have any gig. I was a door man, sure, but I had an instinct to be the best door man there was. It was an atonement every night I stood at the entrance to OAK, heavily inebriated, but with a grateful smile on my face.

I even had a brief fling with a lovely chef from the OAK dessert kitchen.

Shania was a shapely, petite French girl with short blonde hair and green eyes which turned out to be brown in real life – contact lenses.

I bummed a smoke from her one night at the end of shift and we talked about Serge Gainsbourg, which was enough to start whatever we had. I don't recall much of our time together other than how it ended. She went to Dubai with some French friends and met an Irish rugby player, and never came back to London.

It stung when she text me, but it was nothing like anything before. I took it as karma from the times I was unfaithful to Libby.

"I deserved this," I said to myself.

I spent one birthday with Shania during our brief dalliance. I got her a Pokémon cake from the supermarket, nothing special, I wasn't aware that she had any special fondness to Pokémon. I was being playful. When she blew the candles out, she said something very quickly in French, it was her wish, and I know you're not supposed to know the wish, but Shania wasn't the type of lady to adhere to those rules.

"What did you wish for?" I asked.

"I wish to be strong enough to take on anything life throws at me."

That sentiment was everything as very soon I would be tested like never before.

At the start of the week, I woke up to the news all my legal affairs with the band had been resolved, the text message read that I had been 'properly taken care of £££,' which actually, in reality, after tax and legal bills meant diddly squat, but it was still a win. It felt good to be legally single so to speak.

That was the Monday. On the Wednesday, I was halfway through my shift standing in the office aka the bouncer podium by the huge double door entrance to the club. At the time I had my head buried deep into my clipboard, checking in on the night's guest list. It was the standard lot for a Tuesday night: the local elite, art dealers, film people, and of course, the usual nightlife unmentionables. Nothing out of the ordinary. As I emerged from my clipboard, I looked up to see my old friend coincidence in the form of my ex-bandmate Maz standing in front of me with a gaggle of friends wanting to come in. She didn't recognise me at first. I made the most of that and had her escorted in.

I then took a comfort break. I went to the staff bathroom and downed half a bottle of voddie. I then asked one of the club's kitchen staff for a bump of something. The kitchen in any establishment is always the place to go if you need drugs. A cheeky line of coke later and I was back out on my podium, not thinking too much about who I just saw... Well, actually, *all* I was thinking about was who I just saw.

Sometime later I got a tap on my shoulder. It was like Jack Frost touching me. It felt icy and made me judder in revolt. It was Maz.

"I thought it was you, darlin'. How are you?"

I didn't want to speak to her.

I was standoffish. I didn't look at her.

"I been better, Maz."

I had to work. These guests wouldn't let themselves in. I wanted to say fuck off, but my boss was in the vicinity and I needed the job,

"Listen, Pop. I love you, man. I hate that you're working here. I know we never talked after."

She paused, the pause feeling like watching a plastic bag full of shopping fall apart in slow motion. She continued:

"I thought a lot about it, how it must have affected you."

"Not as much as me," I interjected, looking at her square on, our eyes locking. I spoke with enough spite and venom to bring down a T-Rex.

"I'm sure, Pop. We just both saw you change so much with fame. From the kid you started as to who you became was too much for us to handle. We were scared you were going to get so far into the excess that you'd debauch yourself out of a life. Something myself or Vic couldn't accept as enablers. We needed to protect you from you."

I didn't believe a single word she said.

I was drunk and high but could still see through the foggy bullshit.

I croaked with emotion:

"You broke my heart."

Fortunately for me at that exact moment the door got very busy with two *Vianos* of Japanese businessmen wanting to come in. Maz was gone by the time I'd dealt with them.

I didn't see her again. Something I was glad for.

I didn't believe her, getting rid of me was way more about power than proactive compassion. You see, we were all running with our hedonistic rock star lifestyle. It wasn't just me living that way. At the time it was the way everyone at our level was living. It felt like it was more about profit splits than protection. For what it's worth, this is always the *real* reason any band splits up or loses a member.

They call it 'creative differences.'

After these two monumental former band moments following so quickly after each other, I did feel a little closure on the matter of my old musical life. It certainly felt good to tell her how I felt.

That was only the middle of the week.

On the Friday, I woke up late in the afternoon with a banging headache. The moment I turned on my phone, Mum rang. She was screaming. Wherever she was, the background noise was startling: beeps, alarms, a hundred different conversations going on. It sounded like chaos. There was then a fumble, like the phone had been dropped.

Ten seconds later, Dad was on the end of the line. It was now quiet. Dad's voice was clear but he sounded weird.

He would tell me the worst news imaginable: Grandma was in hospital. She'd taken a fall at the cottage; hit her head and lost a huge amount of blood. Dad said the doctors had done all they could do and that she had not long to live.

"Come to the hospital now. Ward F, Room 26B."

I was out on the London cobbles and in a black cab within fifty seconds. My haste was useless. She died ten minutes after the call: one whole hour before I could get there to say goodbye. I didn't know this though as my phone ran out of power a few minutes into the cab journey. Grandma and Grandpa always joked with me how I never kept my phone charged, last time this happened Grandpa would say sarcastically that keeping the phone at five percent makes it work far more efficiently. "Who needs all that juice, Pop? It only slows it down, doesn't it." It was loving sarcasm, not all that toxic shit floating around these days.

On arrival to the hospital I ran straight to the ward almost knocking over a cop escorting a drunk in handcuffs. Grandma, the woman I considered to be my best friend was laying in her hospital bed. She didn't look real. Her light was gone. It was Grandma's body, but something was missing. I had never seen anything like it, the only way to describe was that her fire had gone out, her soul flown away. I got very upset, more upset than I'd ever been. At some point, the porter came to wheel my Grandma's body away. I refused to let them take her. I got confused and couldn't accept that she was gone. Apparently, I was insisting that she was just cold and needed some sugar.

I was convinced this was the case, yet I was clearly in shock. I was screaming for them to bring me "a mother-fucking blanket and an Irn-Bru." Moments later, the same cop I almost ran over earlier appeared with my Dad who had just returned from dropping Mum and Grandpa back in Sleepy Oak. The cop was understanding, and Dad was loving but firm.

"She's gone, mate. She's gone."

His words cut like a knife. The in-denial haze lifted from my vision and acceptance bit me like the cold December morning frost. I looked over to Grandma. I wanted to have one more conversation, just one moment to tell her how much she meant to me. The frosty bite of acceptance stopped me in my tracks. My Grandma had died and this was final.

It was total devastation. My family and I were rocked to our core. Endless tears. We were a collective wreck. Grandpa though... Grandpa completely withdrew. He locked himself away and refused to eat. He began to drink gin like water. Overnight he just let go of life. We all pleaded with him, but he simply refused to look after himself. I found him one night in the observatory. I was there to get stoned and forget. He was there using the telescope to zoom in on constellation 'Jym.' He was very drunk. I had never seen him anything but sober and vice versa. We swapped intoxicants as we shared a moment admiring Grandma's astrological discovery. Grandpa told me he'd been coming out here every night after Grandma's death to look through the telescope. He was convinced he could see Grandma in the stars, waiting for him to join her. With hindsight it was clear that Grandpa knew exactly what he was doing. He told me that he loved me very much, but he was going to meet Grandma up there soon. He wanted to tell me that he and Grandma were always so proud of me. They knew I was currently 'in the wars' but he told me this would be temporary.

"Just like Grandma, your name is in the stars, Pop."

Grandpa then ran his hand through my hair and kissed my forehead.

"I love you, Pop. *We* love you," he said, looking longingly up in the direction of Jym. Sadly, I don't remember how the night ended as we were both out of minds on weed and booze. It's sad because it was the last time I ever saw him alive. Grandpa died two days later. His body was found in the observatory, the telescope set only to one location: Jym. I swear a few nights later I looked in that telescope and I could see them both. I know the weed was strong, but I swear I saw them: the star-crossed lovers were happy to be together again. My heart somehow hurt less after this. There was comfort in knowing they were together again.

Losing them both was the most definitive moment of my adult life. Losing my job in a band paled in comparison.

It was like I had to lose my precious grandparents to understand what a privilege it is to live. Here's a rhetorical question: isn't it a cruel fate that the times when you're living to the hilt you can't appreciate your life with the same sort of gravitas as when you lose someone, or a near-catastrophic accident occurs? It's a cruel twist to a confusing world, isn't it?

For me I understood that I had now hit the ground, probably a lot longer before I would care to admit. I also had a new feeling: it was familiar but distant, unmistakable though. For the first time in a long while I had some fire. I had intention, a little fight. Sure, I had hit the ground hard, but I had absolutely no plans whatsoever to stay there!

Oh yeah, all this happened in December, days before Christmas, Merry Morrison Christmas.

The year – 2008

Subject – Conclusion

Mood – Life

I spent Christmas Day at Sleepy Oak mourning with my parents. In early January, we held a small funeral. My grandparents had been very thorough with how they wanted everything to be done in the event of their death. They didn't want any fuss, or fanfare. It had to be quick with as little stress as possible. They even had a team of pre-paid people with detailed lists of their requests. As part of these requests was that all the contents of their cottage had to be numbered, listed, and boxed ready to put into a storage facility to which only family would ever have access. The observatory would be dismantled and presented to the university where they both studied in Scotland. The cottage would be sold; the proceeds split up into various ways, helping friends, family, and charity.

Myself, Mum and Dad helped with the packing up of the cottage. It was a real bonding experience. We laughed, cried, shared stories. It was symbolic and full of honour, love and respect. This wasn't the last of my symbolic feelings. It was in my grandparent's half-packed away house that I came to the obvious conclusion that I would have to face up to a totally self-created, monstrous mess.

I'd become rather dependent on booze. I was basically a full-blown functioning alcoholic.

It's all fun and games until it isn't.

It took so long for it to compute. Me, an alcoholic? Never.

It's widely documented that the drummer is the liability of any group: the wild one, the one to throw a TV out of a hotel window or drive a Harley Davidson, or in my case, ride a bicycle down hotel corridors.

I read the books. I heard the stories and naively thought that this was all part of the job description. I thought it was my duty to follow in their mischief-making footsteps. It all came naturally. I was happy to try.

The list of my troublemaking examples is endless, yet two instances do come to mind quicker than others, like setting off fireworks onstage. I had these 'petit' things I bought from a motorway service station in France. I knew what I needed to do as soon as I saw the "cherry bombs" looking down at me from the top shelf behind the cash register, my devious drumming 'showman' mind instantly knew I must see what happens if I tape them to my bass drum and let them off during a performance. I thought it would give a good climactic effect to the end of our show.

Well, I successfully and discreetly taped five 'cherry bombs' to my bass drum during a guitar solo interlude. What was unsuccessful, however, was how I totally misjudged the power and range of the things. It literally melted my drum kit and the plastic roof of the outdoor festival we were headlining. It was the last song of the set, so it looked like a wild pyrotechnic Hollywood disaster movie ending, people thought it was all part of the show, but that escapade cost the band's whole festival appearance fee of 250 grand. Oh, it's expensive being 'that' person.

And how about the time I fell asleep drunk in an airplane bathroom causing the plane to make an emergency landing? That was another massive 'band expense!'

With hindsight and fairness to my old musical colleagues, I would have fired myself too. Without even realising, I had become that cliched drummer liability. My alcoholism had become a vicious circle, perhaps even a triangle, a vicious Bermuda triangle that I was completely lost in. Too much time had now passed living this mentally unhealthy lifestyle that it had become all I knew.

I was a functioning addict, but I knew the functioning aspect of my addiction would not stick around forever. I was actually completely sick of myself to the point of no return. All I wanted now was to change.

After finishing up at Sleepy Oak I had to put some distance from London and my self-inflicted toxic routine. I had a little money saved up from working the door and on a whim I wanted to try something I'd never done before, go somewhere I had never been.

Out of all the destinations, India ticked every box. I bought "the tourist bonanza package", as the travel agent guy described it. I flew into Delhi after a long flight sitting three seats in on a very uncomfortable row of five. To try and sleep the journey away I drank miniature bottles of Scottish whisky like Tropicana. This was me winding down: I couldn't just stop and go cold turkey. I felt like I sweated out all my poisons in the first hour in India.

The heat outside Delhi airport was oppressive. The place was not my cup of tea at all: far too many people and not enough air, what air there was tasted like chemical laden exhaust fumes.

A local travel agent rep met me outside, he was holding a piece of scrappy cardboard with POP written in red felt tip.

"Hey mate, I'm Pop," I gasped, sweating furiously.

The young lad led me through the massive crowds and placed me eagerly on a sweltering bus heading to the first of my three Indian get away destinations.

Number one: Agonda, a remote beach town with a tiny population on the edge of the Arabian Sea. It turned out to be the opposite of Delhi, very much my tipple. I had only seen places like this in films or documentaries, there were no traffic lights, no fancy restaurants, Ubers or Pret. I giggled at what looked like the only stipulation, a strict rule of six people minimum to every moped. I loved the community atmosphere: people cooking on open fires everywhere, children playing freely with whatever they could find.

I felt out of place at first but that lasted about ten minutes as the locals were so friendly, they could make anyone feel welcome. With the fresh sea air, the rich luscious green habitat, I was the meat in a bliss sandwich.

The beach sand was pure white and during peak day heat without flip flops it scorched the bottom of your feet. Coconuts lay around in abundance. Their food tasted like pure life, pure health, pure vibes. The hospitality and genuine happiness to just be, was like nothing I had ever experienced, a huge weight left me there. I felt light as air. This is where I was supposed to be.

The plan was to mooch about in Agonda for a week before catching a small prop plane to go see the Taj Mahal, destination number two. I would hang out there for a week before heading off to another beach vibe, with what I hoped would have equal measures of divinity, destination number three.

Destination number two and three never happened.

India is one of those places that insists in no uncertain terms that you DO NOT drink their tap water. They are so strong about this they don't even want you to brush your teeth with it.

I forgot all of this.

Booze does have that effect.

I have a vague memory, in a half semi-conscious alcohol induced state, of quenching my tremendous thirst from the tap in my beach cabana kitchenette after some heavy drinking.

It had been a hell of an evening hanging out by a beach bonfire with the locals and my fellow holiday makers.

The next thing I knew I was jumping out of bed and running to the bathroom, a place I didn't leave for five days straight.

I honestly felt like I had been turned inside out, it was most horrendous.

On the eighth day I felt a little better and emerged from my beach hut infirmary to take a walk. The mood was somber outside, what was wrong?

I asked 'Juwlz' the cabana manager. The day before the town's prop plane and two of my campfire acquaintances had crashed into the side of a mountain in early morning fog heading to the Taj Mahal.

Pure terrification ran through me.

I was supposed to be on that flight.

The next few hours I just walked around mingling with the visibly perplexed locals.

I was extremely thankful for being drunk enough to forget not to drink the tap water. I haven't wanted, needed, or had a sip of alcohol since.

My last drink saved my life.

I stayed put for a few more days and gathered further strength from my inside out tummy-bug-blues before I headed back to Delhi and the first possible flight home. This time I even got upgraded to first class.

POP LUCK!

It would turn out that the rebel attitude I had at school never really left me, and now I used it to rebel against addiction. I used it to prove who's in charge, let my weakened principles know who's the boss. A Herculean task sure, but the reality was I could have been dead, and that thought, for the first time in ages, didn't sit well with me.

I wanted to live. Not only that, I wanted to live well.

Overcoming alcoholism became my sole focus. I wanted to make my family proud and return to being the man and drummer I once was, the man and drummer I was always supposed to be.

I wanted to get back in the hot seat, shake things up like I did when I first arrived on the scene. I wanted to recapture that spirit. It would take me a year to fully shake, rattle and roll my way back to decent, but shake, rattle and roll I did.

PART THREE

The year – 2009

Subject – Grateful

Mood – Sober

(Diary extract)

Energy is as precious as time.
Time and energy can't be bought or sold. They can't be exchanged or returned.
How much we have of both is impossible to gauge, quantify or comprehend.
The only real sage advice to be given on this matter is to spend your
time and energy wisely.
Protect your energy at all costs and value your time like you have
already run out of it.

After I crossed the six-month sober streak I scribbled down these thoughts on a regular basis. Ideas like *Life's not all that bad, is it?* would fly through my mind daily. I was starting to see larger breaks in the dark gloomy Mammatus clouds, and every day this new positivity encouraged a bigger sliver of sun to poke out and shine onto my once weary face. I was beginning to appreciate and revalue what I have in my life, like the ability to truly appreciate the simplicity of a cloud or the joy in silence.

I naturally took all these thoughts and feelings as signs that my spirit was coming back from whatever shitty all-inclusive holiday it had been on.

I even started booking gigs again, just like when I first started out on the scene. I was playing a jazz gig in a nearby pizza restaurant on a Monday, a singer songwriter night in Croydon on the Tuesday, Wednesday a blues jam at a pub in Angel … You get the vibe? I was out there getting involved and having fun to boot. It was an exciting time reconnecting with my instrument and London's vibrant music scene. I was absolutely loving it. I practiced all day and more often than not played a show at night. It was eat, sleep, drum, repeat.

A year into sobriety, my anxiety, panic attacks, and the horror box nightmare had all subsided. My mystery New York book dream even visited me again.

I'd been thinking about it a lot.

When you get sober you do that: you think about your past, you make peace with your mistakes, and you embrace all those good things you have with a deeper sense of appreciation.

The book and the dream were from my old life, but they still felt very special and curiously unfinished.

The latest dream returned on a Sunday afternoon whilst I was sitting on a blue and white striped deck chair on a stoney beach by the river Thames.

I was housesitting for a friend of friend. I'd been shipped in to keep an eye on two very temperamental light grey and lime green parakeets named Binky and Bella. My job was to feed, water and talk to them regularly whilst rubbing the top of their heads at least six times a day wearing a woolly mauve glove. The two birds loved music, specifically soul and classical. Binky would go ape shit for Ludwig van and Bella always piped up with backing vocals to any of Marvin Gaye's soulful catalogue.

I noticed Albee a lot more during this time, perhaps he was jealous.

The house was an enviable place to temporarily call home, perched on the edge of the Thames in Grandma and Grandpa's old stomping ground Greenwich by the Millennium Dome end of the river. It was originally a tea factory, with the faded East India logo still visible.

The old tea factory had an alley running along the side with a thick wrought iron gate at the end which, depending on the tide, could be opened allowing you to walk down a steep set of slippery steps named, "the Pelican Stairs," to a part pebble, part sandy beach. Back in the day, boats would sail all the way up to the tea factory and as the cargo was lowered into the ships the sailors would go and stock up on provisions or grab an ale at the nearest public house. The Pelican Stairs and the alley were their passage to and from.

The dream returned on a Sunday. I know this because that was the day the parakeets got a whole mango each to chomp on. Sandy had installed in her cellar a supermarket size freezer which was filled solely with mangoes and every Saturday you took two out in anticipation for what I imagined was the birds' favourite day of the week. Sandy would always call on Saturday evenings to remind me of this very important task.

It was definitely a Sunday because I had just put out Bella and Binky's special Sunday lunch mangoes and I was heading out to the part pebble, part sandy beach with a blue and white stripy deckchair to catch some rays and fresh air.

As I looked out in a relaxed daze to the majestic river, the way the sun was hitting the water reminded me of a huge mirror ball. Watching this soothed me slowly into a peaceful trance.

"Oi, you, soft arse, I'm locking the gate, you staying here all night, are ya?"

I woke with a jolt, the sun was blinding, all I could see was the dark silhouette of a massive geezer in front of me. I didn't want to be there all night – or even right there and then for that matter. I was up in a jiffy, deck chair under arm and an apology in action.

I needed to get back sharpish anyway. I had something very important to write down. My river doze had somehow helped stir up my discovery of Drewford Alabama's book in room 613 at The Gershwin Hotel, and as I climbed the Pelican Stairs it dawned on me.

"They have all been dreams, Pop."

I laughed at the absurdity of my reoccurring theme dream.

"They were clearly all dreams, man." I said with a raised voice, that was more like a polite shout. The slight echo from the cold stone stairs and the surrounding tall London brick buildings made the statement more real.

"They were all dreams, were they mate?" the big cockney chap said sarcastically as he passed me on the slippery steps.

I didn't respond. My mind was off to the races. It made me think of Grandpa's dreams are like oranges metaphor. It made me wonder what the hell was going on in my mind, *What are you trying to tell me, Drewford Alabama?*

This Sunday afternoon 'recurring dream' picked up right where all the others did, and as before I was left with a brand-new sentence and mysterious duo of letters. I wrote down the newest additions to my ever-expanding cryptic conundrum collection.

This dream provided me with, 'DONT FORGET,' along with the 'E, O.'

Yet again, it made no sense.

Once finished, I went for a run along the river. This was my new obsession, and I must say combined with quitting booze had contributed massively to some significant weight loss. I was in a great place. I felt amazing about my appearance and more importantly within myself.

I made peace with my natural big-boned plus size, or rather what I imagined others thought about my plus size. I realised I didn't give a fuck. Ultimately, I concluded that it doesn't matter, because when you're living life with those goggles on there is no size or look that will satisfy you. There's no end game on that road, just a circular pattern of self-hate which only ends with more madness and sadness.

I had been through a lot. It was also very clear that my life was very different now. I looked different, I felt different and for good reason all I needed was somewhere different to live.

I was actively looking for places. I knew looking after Binky and Bella was only going to be a temporary privilege, and the Kings Cross house share had run its course with all the kids now fully fledged bankers on the cusp of enjoying six figure salaries.

London was still going to be home. I had zero plans to leave just yet. But which part of the city I should relocate to? The whole of London had been my stomping ground. I had ravaged the entire capital, tried, and tested all its different variations and varieties. With all that insight I decided that there's no better place to reside than slap bang in the middle of it, and fortunately that's exactly where I would find myself.

I ended up moving into a large rough and tumble flat above a music shop on a significant road in Soho: Denmark Street.

The rent was high, but Grandma and Grandpa had left me some money on the proviso it was used to get me back 'up and running' not to be squandered on 'alcohol or other unmentionables'. This was precisely the opposite: this was investing. I wanted to treat myself to a new exciting living experience. I hoped being in a place where I really wanted to be would encourage further positivity.

I was over the moon with my new accommodation. I managed to bag the whole expansive top floor above Kinsey's piano and synthesiser emporium.

I was given a two-year lease and didn't even have to put a deposit down or pay the water and electricity bills. I didn't question the generosity!

For the second time in my life, I hit the London accommodation jackpot.

I had my own space, my new rock and roll wigwam for my very new self.

I could leave my drum kit set up 24/7 and make all the racket I wanted whenever I wanted. I even had my own roof terrace with a view of the city, where I would grow orchids in a dome shaped green house that had been there since the 60s. A private outdoor sanctuary in central London is very rare and I made the absolute most of it. I adored sitting out there with the sunset and my thoughts.

I was right on the edge of buzzing Soho that I could not only see, but feel its radiant glow from my new home. My new nesty hovel was most revitalising particularly as it held that hefty wedge of symbolic significance from formative years working for Tommy at the drum shop.

In the process of moving to my new digs I rediscovered the flame-scorched sweetie tin. It was packed away like a Russian doll, hidden inside a bag within a bigger bag within a bigger bag.

It seemed that I had accumulated a lot of baggage, literally and metaphorically. The day I finished moving in, I laid the final and most special sweetie tin bag on the creaky wooden floorboards in the centre of the open plan New York loft-inspired flat and went about removing all the items from within: a pair of drum sticks, a cream-coloured poncho, hotel slippers, a few other unmemorable items, until there it was, in all its glory: the flame-scorched tin.

Overcome with excitement, I couldn't wait and pulled off the lid and gently lifted out the Gershwin hotel towel parcel and unwrapped the soft white bundle revealing the beaten-up old book.

"You have spent far too long hiding," I said.

Holding the book in front of me, I examined it like I had never done before.

"We have both been through so much."

I spent the rest of the afternoon perusing the pages, the words and sketches resonating with me very differently from ever before. I was a lot older now, I had experienced life's rollercoaster ride way more than the naive kid who first came across the book.

Now the words felt like they were written for me, as if Drewford Alabama was writing about me.

That night my dream returned, and like the others it was accompanied with another new cryptic message.

"THE MIDDLE." and "N, E."

I had quite a collection by now.

I was spellbound by this Drewford Alabama, the thought of him would not leave my mind.

Who was he?

Where was he?

I took it upon myself to find out.

It became my personal high priority mission to learn all I could about this man.

From his work, I assumed him to be an artist of some stature. I imagined I'd stumbled across a famous artist's private notebook. A glance into a popular author's inner thoughts perhaps? I began asking around to see if people had heard of him.

"Drewford who?" Being the constant disappointing answer.

When my searches online led to nothing I soon realised I was FAR too confident in my ability to locate this mysterious Alabama, and time, as it usually does, began to pass. But as the months went by my Drewford Alabama obsession only grew stronger.

I believed I had found a rare diamond, and it was frustrating that his name and writings were not widely known. It very much felt like they should.

My obsession with the book and Mr Alabama were given a glimmer of hope when I saw an advert for a company who specialise in tracing back and discovering your family tree. It was like a jigsaw falling into place in my mind, I was fizzing. I'd had a magnificent idea!

Later that day I paid fifty buckeroos to F.T.F USA (family tree finder), under the name of Alfie Alabama!

It was a bare-faced lie, but it sounded good.

I gave F.T.F one piece of information:

"My nearest known family member is Drewford Alabama from the United States of America."

I set up a brand-new email account and assigned a different sound for incoming email – a series of church bells escalating in tone ending in a climatic crash cymbal hit.

Majestic!

I waited and waited for those ecclesiastical sounds to return to my ears, but they never did. After six months I sent an email to the account to check it was still working.

Mic check one-two, one-two was the 'subject.'

I pressed send and Ten seconds later those church bells rang out.

Disappointment was the word.

Time passed and I began to think it was a lost cause. Fortunately, Drewford's words were liquid poetry to me, more than enough to keep me enthused. The dream even returned for the sixth time, I was convinced there was a bigger message, something important. The dream never got old – reliving the book's discovery, my face lighting up when I held it in my hand, putting the book to my nose to smell it – would always fill my head with sweet reminiscence.

I couldn't put my finger on the disappearing ink and the ghostly cryptic writings, all I knew was tracking down Drewford Alabama would be my best chance to find out. I decided to hire a private investigator to dig a little deeper than the standard channels on the internet.

One of the lot I used to hang out with in my belligerent days, a B-list television presenter with a penchant for sleeping with fans, had worked with a private detective to track down a stalker she'd picked up through all her shenanigans. It was clear that it meant a lot less to her than it did to him as this crazy dude would not leave her alone, turning up at work, her home, even parties, the pub, and the park. She was getting scared, and on the advice of her management team, got a private detective in to gather enough evidence that the police had to intervene. Well, the PI tracked down the sneaky stalker within the week. The following week the police had all the information needed to throw a caution on the guy. After that, he disappeared. She never saw him again.

I saw the PI method work for her. There was no reason it wouldn't work for me.

It was a costly solution, but results speak for themselves. These detectives have ways the ordinary citizen would struggle to comprehend, gizmos and gadgets, friends in high and low places, it's all a bit 'men in black', a bit hush hush.

Mr Detective began his dossier on Mr Alabama. The word 'dossier' made it instantly feel like progress was happening. This alone justified the £800 expense, especially if it got me closer to Mr Drewford Alabama.

After signing a bunch of papers, I had an immense craving for falafel, luckily West London has the best spot for this type of culinary itch in the form of a little hut at the entrance to Shepherd's Bush market.

Woody the proprietor of this miniature eatery has always run his place with pride and enthusiasm. He's a real gem of a man. If you ever get a chance to go tell him Pop sent you, he will slip you an extra falafel.

A quick bite at Woody's then back to Denmark Street to play drums, it was samba Saturday, my day of the week to brush up on all my Latin grooves. A brilliant day if ever I heard of one.

By early evening I was suitably drummed out and happily sitting out on the terrace, writing in my diary whilst sipping on a lovely steaming cup of Moroccan whisky.

The thought of false trophies swirled round my head, those things without substance that only bring on a morish endorphin rush.

As I wrote I smiled because the words showed me how much progress I had made.

(Diary extract)

'False Trophies,' I think that any human with a mantlepiece full of such false trophies is no happier than the human without, the pursuit of chasing false trophies and the power they wield ravages the human spirit, its devastation akin to drug addiction,

I laid the pen down to rest on top of the notebook and finished my tea. I didn't know it yet, but an unexpected twist to my day was about to occur. It began on one of my evening walks. Since getting sober I found great joy in walking without intention. London is a phenomenal city for such a thing, it's a place that never ceases to surprise in revealing new unexplored areas of interesting history, architecture, quirk, or character.

This evening it was the latter that caught my attention. I heard an unmistakable sound.

It was a laugh. A laugh that made me smile the moment I heard it. A laugh I was certain I knew the 'character' it was attached to. I back tracked my steps trying to locate the culprit. I was positive I knew the source, yet I had to see it to believe it. It was toasty in London that night and the pubs had overflowed with drinkers spilling out on to the streets, taking over the pavement and surrounding roads. It's always an endearing sight of great merriment, and in my prime I have no doubt that I would have been right in the mix causing havoc and entertaining the masses. That evening I weaved anonymously in and out of the sauced-up Londoners until I saw the source of the unmistakable cackle.

There he was in all his glory.

My ears were not deceiving me. This marvellously, unexpected moment was no illusion. Without further ado, may I reintroduce into this chapter of my life, Mr Pauly DiMaggio the most New York man I ever met.

Pauly was standing there, cigarette in his left hand, pint in the right whilst entertaining two ladies who were completely enamoured in his presence. It was a most excellent sight. I made my way through the cheery London drinkers to Pauly D.

As I got closer, we locked eyes.

"Excuse me sir, you probably won't remember, but you once drove me from Newark Airport to the Gershwin Hotel in Manhattan."

Before I finished my reintroduction Pauly cut me off.

"Cor blimey governor," he said in a mock English accent showing off that memorable shiny gold tooth smile of his.

"English, course I remember you, I am standing right here because of you kid," he said as he pulled me in for a hug.

"How's that Pauly?" I responded after our embrace.

"It's you who suggested I follow my dream of being a stand-up comedian, it's you who without knowing it gave me the final push I needed. Your encouragement to follow my dreams and your clear passion for what you were doing was just the kick up the ass I was missing. I finished taxi driving two days later. I had enough dough saved up to give it a good six month go. If it didn't work out at least I could say to myself I tried. You remember what you told me Pop?"

"What's that Pauly?"

"Fortune favours the bold, brother.

"On the fifth month, with less than two weeks of money left to my name, a major talent agent spotted me. They were there to see some shmo performing after me, for whatever reason shmo was running late so I took his slot. That was it baby, they signed me up. I started warming up the audience for the big acts until I made my way up through the ranks to where I am here today. I just completed a residency at a small comedy club down the street, or 'road' as you Brits call it, it's official, I'm now in the business of making people laugh. I get triple the bread for half the work, and you know what? I love it. What you drinking English? Let's celebrate our reunion. It's like the fuckin' Beatles getting back together, only we like each other! Capeesh?"

For posterity, he documented the reunion with a selfie of us, and we hung out for a couple more hours, until his two ladies became one and without a word, he surreptitiously walked into the night with her on his arm.

I never saw the photograph Pauly and I took, we didn't even swap numbers or emails. That's fine, we probably will bump into each other again someday. I like it that way, fate and faith in spontaneity.

I watched an episode or two of Pauly's show on YouTube and he had me in complete stitches and to his credit he had millions of views and subscribers. Turns out he had changed his name to Pauly Kemosabe and started a podcast in which he talks about his early days in New York as a cab driver slash coke dealer. This was news to me, but it explains how his eyes looked like a robber's dog.

I'm sure not all his viewers got their first taste of his wicked humour from the back of a yellow taxi, but if he really was this hot shot mobile cocaine supplier perhaps people did, it starts to make sense now.

The next few weeks and months flew by. As they did, my desire to know more about Mr Alabama continued to grow.

Each week I would check in with the PI and every time there was nothing new to report.

"It's as if this guy never existed Pop. I have my people working on it in America, but they're stumped too. I could keep taking your money, mate, but it seems to be a non-starter."

Man was I disappointed; I really thought my team of Sherlocks could dig up the information I craved.

I would let out my frustrations by bashing away at the drums for a few hours at a time. Once played out I would visit my diary, there was nothing more cathartic, both acts for me seemed to go hand in hand.

I began to write to Mr Alabama himself, he'd become a pen pal of sorts, more of a therapist really. In my letters I told him both exciting and mundane things about navigating my new life.

Nothing and everything. It was also a way to feel less lonely. I had lost all my so-called friends in the fall out, the few I had left were rarely around. I certainly wasn't going out my way to make any effort with the whole 'friendship' thing. Associates, sure. Colleagues, certainly. Friends? Not so much.

Mum understood too. She suggested I got a dog: man's best friend she said. Well, man did need a friend. I really didn't need much more convincing than that. Roscoe was a shy little red-haired, baggy faced chow-chow with the most stunning emerald-green eyes you've ever seen. This number one *stunna* arrived from the shelter as a tiny puppy, and my oh my, was his precious puppy presence a most welcome addition to my life.

Before Roscoe was Roscoe he came with a very different title, over at the old cat and dog shelter he was affectionately known as Snaggletooth. A supremely accurate name if you're just judging his gnashers, but to me he was just CUTE A F.

I thought Snaggletooth was a bit like calling someone 'big boned', so my puppy's name changed on first sight. Now he's Roscoe, Roscoe Morrison.

So there we were, me, Roscoe and my fragile orchids flourishing beautifully in my sentimental Denmark Street home. With all this positivity I had so much to say, so many thoughts and ideas, things to do, places to see and emotions I felt.

I was filling my diaries at quite a rate.

Every few weeks I wrote to Drewford Alabama, my unofficial therapist.

Drewford,

Things continue to get better by the day. I don't miss alcohol one bit, in fact I feel like I've finally broken free from some invisible shackles which have been holding me back for years.

Today I have been thinking about life, now I don't know why but I really feel like you would totally get where I am coming from.

Life is like water!

Life is the water in a stream which we are all privileged to be flowing down.

After our journey is over the water in the stream will continue moving and life will carry on. Because our presence in the river of life is fleeting it's highly important to travel it in a way that makes you happiest.

The bits that don't mean anything positive let go of, and the pieces that bring you joy hold dear.

Some would say that there's no rhyme or reason as to what makes one's life journey successful, for me I believe we do have a say.

For instance, there is no doubt that positivity and good vibrations are self-incited in much the same way as the opposite, these are powerful forces in life never to be underestimated.

Because you can never be sure what's round the next corner, I am going to be sure to travel my journey with good intentions and sincerity, I will do this by being true to myself and following my heart, spending my time and energy on the things I love most and forever keeping myself open to the possibility of the unexpected.

If I can't live my best life just yet I will continue to shimmy and shake myself into a position where I can.

Fortune favours the bold.

Drewford, I have come to the conclusion that this is living a good life in the truest sense.

Do mind your feet as there are two broken shackles on the floor!

In other news,

I had another dream!

They seem to be more frequent now, as if they are leading to something, it's a sort of surreal hilarity that in all these years never once have they made sense!

As usual the dream came with a new message: "IS FOR YOU" followed by "W, I."

As it's all close to gibberish in my mind, something is telling me that tracking you down is key to giving these conundrums clarity, but gee wiz Mr Alabama you're a hard man to find.

I am not going to give up though that's for sure!

That's all from me today Drewford. Roscoe my little puppy dog is currently barking incessantly in the next room. Until next time buddy.

Love Pop

Year – 2009

Location – Denmark Street

Mood – Amazed

S omething rather miraculous happened!
I was on my roof top terrace playing an all-white acoustic guitar that came with the flat. This guitar had what you would call in the business of music 'charm', which is another way of saying it wasn't great. Truthfully, when it came to guitar-playing I wasn't that great either, so I figured we were pretty much a match made in six-string heaven.

I was teaching myself how to play some tricky bluesy minor chords, a task which was going reasonably well until my concentration was temporally broken by church bells ringing from inside the flat. It took a few moments, but when I realised the bells were emanating from my open laptop everything clicked into place.

There was a message accompanying the sound: 'YOU HAVE MAIL.'

A most splendid sight indeed.

I had received an email from 'F.T.F Family Tree Finder Service.'

Those bells I selected to chime were now majestically ringing throughout my flat providing me with a feeling of great delight. I immediately logged in to see what was waiting for me.

CONGRATULATIONS ALFIE
You have 23 Alabamas related to you.
1 living.
NAME: M Alabama
LOCATION: Poughkeepsie, New York, USA

Intrigued I clicked further to see Alfie's deceased relations.

This is when I believe over time my connection to the book had tapped me into a higher Alabama power, because when I saw Drewford

Alabama's name at the top of the list I was not a bit surprised. I knew instinctively he wasn't with us any longer, even though I could feel his presence.

Later when I took Roscoe out for our evening walk, I thought about M Alabama. I wondered what relation they had to Drewford. I could feel that even though Drewford was far, far away, I was somehow getting closer.

With the F.T.F lead, within a mere matter of weeks I tracked down M Alabama.

M was for Mary. Mary Ann Alabama from Poughkeepsie, New York. Drewford Alabama's widowed wife.

Mary had a couple of social media pages with a few friends and followers apiece, she was clearly a tech savvy senior. It was simple. I dropped her a message and explained what I'd discovered. Mary was totally up for chatting online, so I wasted no time in explaining exactly how I found one of her husband's books. I tried my absolute best to express how much Drewford's tattered pages meant to me. It turns out I found this quite hard to do over messenger, perhaps I was nervous, all I knew is I wasn't my best. My words just couldn't match the feeling.

I thought about how meeting Mary in person would be great: to be able to talk to her in 'analogue,' ask her questions and hear stories about her life with Mr Alabama. On the spur of the moment, I suggested exactly that, to which she instantly declared it to be "a capital idea Mr Morrison."

I was so excited to hear more about the man behind the words – words I had been obsessing over for so long.

I was thrilled. Mary was keen to meet me, and she was eager to see Drewford's book. It was all arranged and in late summer, exactly six weeks after our first exchange, I shipped Roscoe off to Bella and Binky (as in the spoilt Parakeets) while I flew to New York City for another expedition.

I didn't lose my bag this time round, but something else was gone. My old friend Gershwin.

The place changed hands a few times in quick succession, the last owner running its legacy into the ground. Now it's the head office to the world's most popular dating app.

With the Gershwin gone I stayed with a friend of Binky and Bella's guardian in the financial district. When I first arrived at the Wall Street apartment, I was greeted by a man who referred to himself only as, 'the owner.' He was a sight to behold. He didn't look like 'the owner' of such a fancy place, that's for sure, but this was a healthy reminder for me not to judge a book by its cover. Our owner guy was wearing a Hawaiian shirt and very tight shiny gold shorts. He had a baggy leather waistcoat over his shirt – with a difference. The waistcoat front pockets were fur-lined, each one containing a tiny puppy. The canines were happily hanging out, their small heads and paws poking out of their ickle puppy pouch pockets like adorable Christmas decorations.

Another of the 'owner's' many intriguing features was his pink freezer bag. He paused to open the bag which turned out to be choc-a-bloc full of blue ice lollies, which as our time together continued, he consumed at a very fast pace, fast enough for me to notice his lips going blue right before my eyes. Every time he unwrapped a new lolly, he cheerily shared it with the pups who gladly licked away in a frenzy seemingly knowing all too well it was only a matter of time before 'the owner' would take back command of the iced treat.

'The owner' was bald with grey designer stubble and Michael Caine style thick rimmed glasses homing two beady dark brown eyes. On each hand he was sporting a chunky gold Cuban link bracelet, and on his feet were gleaming, box-fresh Nike air Jordans.

This look was extra-extra.

It wasn't a weird or scary scene. Clearly a man doing exactly what he wanted to do. NFG. *No fucks given.*

As he took me through the building, Bossa Nova music was blaring at a high volume from a huge Notting Hill carnival style speaker system at the end of the lobby. I couldn't help noticing bowls of what looked like sugar, bulbs of garlic, and cinnamon sticks on every windowsill.

Curious.

Without stopping, he pointed to a kitchen and bathroom area, I barely caught a glimpse of either. Soon we approached a weirdly long and very thin hallway decorated in Vogue magazine front covers. At the end of the hallway, there were two doors facing each other: one painted turquoise, the other neon pink. He opened the neon pink one to the right stating, "This will be your room." As the door screeched open, he lit an extra-long match procured from a bum bag.

The owner immediately held the match away from the pups and pointed into the room aiming the light of the burning flame into the dark space. This was on account of the lights being "busted".

"No problem," I responded.

With his match providing the only light flickering away in his hand, he gestured to a selection of match boxes on the bedside table and pointed to countless empty wine bottles dotted around the room with half spent candles sticking out of them.

No words, just an unspoken dialogue I was now fully tuned into.

As the match got close to burning his fingers, he sped up his pace, and with what I predicted to be less than thirty seconds of lit match time remaining, he explained that it was "a quiet week at the ranch, with just a couple from Europe staying in the main room and an Australian photographer shooting graffiti in the abandoned subway stations at night."

The owner gestured towards the turquoise door opposite.

"It's a doozy!" he announced.

"What's a doozy?" I had to ask.

"It's real good," he responded with an exasperation I sensed he very much enjoyed.

To me this place felt edgy and vibrant. I loved it. Nothing like the Gershwin. Nothing like anything I'd ever experienced. In the final moments of the match's glow, the owner opened the drawer from a vintage school desk inside the room containing lots of keys and ketchup sachets.

"You will work it out," he said. "Leave the money here with the keys when you leave."

With that he flamboyantly flicked his wrist in a style from the old movies and, in a cloud of match smoke, he disappeared into the sounds of Bossa Nova never to be seen again.

Turns out 'the owner' owned all five floors of the building. In the late 70s and 80s he was an agent for a super famous artist. I imagined Warhol. After meeting the European couple, I got chatting with Dylan the photographer, who was staying in the room opposite me. Perhaps I found him boring as, two minutes in, I felt the first wave of sleep hit quick and sharp like a freshly tuned drum. It was time to head down the narrow Vogue lined catwalk to my neon pink doored dorm to light a few candles and fall asleep

Oh, those weird bowls dotted all over the place? The German couple told me that they are to ward off bad vibes.

When it comes to expelling bad vibes, I say anything is worth a shot.

The recipe? Salt, garlic cloves, cinnamon sticks all in a bowl placed beside your front door or windows. Bad vibes be gone. Allegedly.

My inner detective told me the light bulbs probably never shone in my room. You could barely see the bottles for the huge mounds of multi-coloured candle wax dripped and dried like some sort of heroin-chic art installation.

That night, as I lay in bed, I put my headphones on, and listened to a collection of nature sounds from the Brazilian rainforest. Just before drifting off the fully blown responsible adult I had now become blew out the candles and finally checked out for the day.

In the middle of the night, I was woken up abruptly with the very real sensation that somebody had shaken me awake. This was a second-ary thought and once awake the important thing was that I'd had another Drewford Alabama dream. The recurring dream had once again reoccurred, only this time back in New York where it all began. How apt. With the room midnight black, I proceeded to use my mobile phone's electric glow to guide me to the nearest box of matches where I lit one of the many dripped candle bottle art beacons.

I really liked the room drenched in this type of light. There wasn't one bit of discomfort for the lack of the modern convenience that is electricity. I wondered whether this was the reason the lights hadn't been fixed yet. I wouldn't have fixed them yet either.

I took great joy in writing by the glow of candles, it added a whole new level of special to the mysteriousness of my dream and inevitably the usual accompanying messages, this time my weird cryptic gifts were "THE END" and "S, H."

In the moment I was too 'positively stirred' to interpret "THE END" negatively. It was just strange. After finishing scribbling, I lay my pencil down and less responsibly fell back asleep basking in the moody glow of candlelight.

The next day I woke up well and, as intended, I eagerly caught the train from Grand Central Station to Poughkeepsie. Guess who was already there to meet me on the platform: Albee, buzzing around in a sea of pigeons.

"Yes, mate," I said in full poshney with a wide smile. Everything felt right.

During the two- and half-hour journey sitting in my spacious seat on a very pleasant train, I wrote down all my questions for Mary. It was a super-hot day. My section of the train had a lovely breeze rolling through it from the tiny open widows at the end of each carriage. It was an idyllic journey. I had the locomotive space mostly to myself, bar a few stops when I shared the carriage with some hyper kids dressed to the nines in army gear, some sort of 'Cub Scout' American alternative I concluded.

I purposely arrived in Poughkeepsie an hour before I arranged to be at Mary's so I could soak it all in, take in the sights: cool, calm and collected.

I bought myself a tropical ice lolly from the ice cream truck outside the station to assist me in this. As I tasted that frozen treat in the glorious Poughkeepsie sun, I thought how the simplest of life's pleasures are always the most overlooked, and I made a point of writing this insight down: IT'S THE SIMPLE THINGS.

An ice lolly on a hot sunny day couldn't be more perfectly splendid if it tried. "So good a bee will sting you for it," the ice cream vendor weirdly said as I passed him some bucks. I wrote that line down too.

I pulled the shades hanging from my open shirt and set them in their designated place on my nose in preparation for getting my Poughkeepsie day going, and with iced treat in one hand and briefcase in the other I was more than ready to set off to meet Miss Mary Ann Alabama.

Here's a fact about Poughkeepsie. Scrabble the popular board game was created here, this makes sense to be honest. I wondered what must it feel like to be the inventor of such a thing? To make something that resonates so deeply in the world of board games. Makes me think, do we ever really know where an idea can lead to? Could the only valuable creative lesson in life be that following through with an idea is the only currency we truly have to trade in? It's pure wonder stuff and if it wasn't already clear already, I should point out that the Wonderboy had now absolutely, definitely, returned.

As I started my final approach to Miss Mary Alabama's house, I studied the other houses on rather appropriately named Grand Drive: all nice, freshly painted, manicured lawns, every other house flying the star-spangled banner.

"Patriotic road," I said out loud, perhaps to Albee. I am sure he was close by.

As I got further down, I spotted the great lady herself Miss Mary Alabama sitting in the vast porch of her home. She was sitting in a pink rocking chair enjoying her view of the magnificent Poughkeepsie day. When I got close enough Mary gently waved to me.

"Come on over, Pop."

My memory goes in slow motion as I pushed the white picket fence gate open and followed the short path up to her house, the whole time taking in the immaculate, vibrantly multi-coloured garden that complemented the house with its bright white and baby blue trim.

It looked like a doll's house: the stained-glass windows, the garden. It was like a picture-perfect postcard. I was sure I'd seen it before.

On arrival I introduced myself to Mary, a mere formality as we began to chat like old friends. She welcomed me like family. I brought a Dictaphone tape recorder with me. To me it was like interviewing a political dignitary or a Hollywood star. I wanted to document the moment with a recording. Mary thankfully agreed. I am so relieved she did as I used the tapes considerably when recalling our conversation for this story.

Mary turned out to be an absolute firecracker, sharp as a nail and quick as a fox.

She had short soft grey hair with two red clips keeping her bangs from her eyes, her skin was smooth and radiant. Two big pearl earrings hung from her ears and she was sporting a rather nifty pale yellow lipstick, proper swinging sixties style. She was beautiful.

Her engagement ring was a stunning red ruby stone set in a slim gold band, and as we spoke the ruby glistened in endless variations under the hot sun. It was hard not to notice the sweet-smelling alabaster-coloured roses planted nearby, whimsically exciting the senses further in short, sweet, light breezy blasts.

After talking up a storm for an hour or so there was a natural lull in conversation.

I took this moment to show Mary the book. Drewford's book.

"I remember these," she said enthusiastically.

The sight of it immediately jump-started our chat back into top gear.

"He had so many of them. I offered to buy him a typewriter, but he wasn't having it. He loved pen on paper, loved the effort. He filled these books at a great rate. Drewford loved writing stories, poems, drawing pictures, trouble was he never had the courage to do anything with them, but perhaps that was the point, maybe it was all for him, maybe that was enough.

Drew was sure enough a loquacious man. He had an endless imagination."

At this point I averted my gaze in reaction to her choice of words, something she noticed immediately.

"Loquacious means chatty, Pop."

She smiled. Her eyes endearingly closing, just like an affectionate cat.

"He used to say one of his hobbies was meeting people, and I would say that's not a hobby just part of living. He disagreed and always maintained that writing in his books, taking care of his garden, and chatting with strangers were his hobbies."

I couldn't believe what she was saying. Not only did I feel the same way about pen to paper, but since I'd got sober my hobby for chit chat had returned with full force.

"ME TOO," I blurted.

"What's that Pop?"

"I have to say Mary, I'm with Drewford on the hobby of conversation."

"Are you now?" she half-laughed with her adorable half-closed cat eyes.

The conversation was going great, way better than I expected.

I was loving listening to Mary speak and she seemed keen for me to re-tell my story on how Drewford's prized notebook ended up in my possession. I gladly obliged. I told her all about the lost luggage, the damaged lining of my thrift store tartan suitcase, the band, the come up, the fire, the success, getting sacked, my grand-parents, India, getting sober and last but certainly not least, the dreams. I declared his book to be in my possession by way of coincidence, fate, and luck.

"A veritable happy accident, perhaps even a miracle," I said with extra enthusiasm.

"Happy accident is a splendid double word summary," Mary proclaimed. "A miracle? Well, I don't know about that Pop, but I believe Drewford would have said the very same thing. He believed in miracles too."

She chuckled softly. I joined in the giggles, only stopping to admire a stunning, amber-tinted butterfly that chose the table in front of us to rest. Gazing trance-like at the creature she concluded: "You and Drewford are just like that butterfly – sweet optimists."

"Sweet optimists," I repeated as the butterfly took off to pastures new.

Mrs Alabama paused for a long moment before speaking again.

"Well, it seems to me Pop that you were supposed to find Drewford's notebook, perhaps anyone else would have passed it by as just another book with someone's rambling scribbles written within, not for what it could be. It takes a certain person to see something for what it really is Pop. Drewford had that same gift. That's another similarity I've counted between you and him. This book here is extra special because you found it. I want you to keep the book Pop. I know Drewford would want that too, do with it what you like."

Then we sipped flowery jasmine tea accompanied by cucumber sandwiches and carrots from the garden accompanied with a hummus-like dip brought to us all by a lady called Ellie.

"Here, I fixed you a plate. The amount of talking you're both doing, I'm sure you've worked up an appetite."

I wasn't expecting jasmine tea and cucumber sandwiches to be such a harmonious accompaniment for the moment.

Ellie lived at the house, helping Mary whose impressive sharpness wasn't enough to hide the fact she was incredibly old, or as Mary put it, 'a woman of a certain vintage.'

Ellie had one blue eye and one brown eye, just like David Bowie.

I told her I thought it looked fabulous.

She didn't know that Bowie also shared this unique trait which I was most happy to tell her. Ellie asked me in a soft voice, "Was he the man from space?"

"Yes, he was indeed Ellie. THE STAR MAN."

Feeling the good buzz of quality company, we continued talking about Drewford, or Drew as Mary called him. The redundant scrunched up notes I made on the train staying firmly in my pocket. Our conversation was flowing like the jasmine tea from its large lime green and white polka dot teapot.

It turned out Mary had been an English teacher and Drewford worked in public services somewhere within Grand Central Station.

"Drew was a jack of all trades. He liked to get his hands dirty, liked to get things done. He was a popular guy and the bosses at the station valued him highly. He was a huge asset to them." Mary continued, "He was one of four general managers and often took care of five or six jobs at a time. This suited Drew just fine. He loved working at the station very much and would often say it was the best job in the city. He absolutely adored how every single week was different and on any given day you would never know what captivating sight you would see, or what interesting person you would meet. It was a constant merry-go-round of new events and remarkable occurrences. I think these are what a lot of his writings were based on."

It seems the two hard-working Alabamas also liked their respective jobs for another reason. Drewford's workday would end before Mary's, which was ideal, because on his journey home he passed the school where Mary worked just as her teaching day ended. Drewford would stand by the school gates as she walked out and once reunited, they would walk home holding hands while sharing stories of their day's endeavours.

Mary made a point of telling me that this is exactly what they did as childhood sweethearts. They both attended different schools at the opposite ends of town, but once they started courting in the last year of compulsory education, Drewford would skip the final twenty minutes of his last class of the day so he would have enough time to cycle over and meet Mary at her school gates. The same school where, as a girl, she once played hopscotch. She eventually became the principal.

Such beautiful vibes.

Mary also told me how they had a habit of wearing matching clothes. Whether it was as minor as a hat or jacket, or as much as head-to-toe matching suits, these twinned love birds were unmissable, walking down the street holding hands, smiling, and chatting. The Alabama couple, just like my grandparents, sweethearts, best friends, and husband and wife.

A trilogy of meant-to-be-love.

While Ellie was watering the thirsty garden flowers with a purple watering can, Mary asked her to bring down the photograph from her bedside table. As we were talking about him so much, Mary wanted him to be sitting on the table with us.

"The butterfly seat," she said with a smile.

Whilst Ellie was upstairs Mary went on to astonish me, as if our last couple hours of conversation were just a warm-up.

She continued, "He loved telling me about who he met or what he heard every day. Often, I couldn't comprehend it all as his energy and imagination were relentless. His stories, ideas and opinions, well, it was all so special. I was just happy to be with him, to be entertained by whatever event or encounter Drewford wanted to tell me about. It was so fortunate that Drewford's workplace offered such a mixture of opportunities for him. The thing about New York City is no one really lives there, only the super wealthy or those who haven't worked it out yet. You commute, darling," she said with an upper Hamptons twang. "If you want a garden, and if you want space, peace and quiet, it's simple. You get more bang for your buck, that's for sure." Mary continued, "There was no bigger station in the city and if you lived out of town, well then. The chances are you went through Grand Central to get there, and if you did, it's very likely Drew would begin to recognise you. He was remarkable at remembering a face my Drewford was," Mary then stared off, in a dream, I imagine thinking about her sorely missed partner in crime. "I remember he even managed to strike up a friendship with a famous movie actor who would feed the pigeons at the end of platform twelve every morning when he was in the city working. Drew would often talk of his conversations with this Hollywood star. I recall they were always about politics, fishing or bitching out his co-stars. When Drewford died the actor came to visit me after the funeral."

"Who was he Mary? What movies was he in?" I asked in quick succession.

"Oh, now you got me! I can't remember the movies Pop. I was never one for cinema really. I always preferred a good book. Apparently, he once played a gladiator or something along those lines."

"Hollywood royalty that's for sure," Ellie chipped in.

Mary moved on:

"Drewford met many people from many walks of life, he liked to keep tabs on all of them, especially the people he deemed 'important folk,' the dignitaries, the politicians. There was a mistress to a host of powerful New York big wigs."

Mary paused as if reminded of something important, and I took this time to sip some tea and chew uninterrupted on crunchy sweet carrots and a cool refreshing 'cu-cu' sandwich.

Mary continued, "Oh lovely, sweet, beautiful Hyacinth." Mary recalled this lady with a smile and as she beamed under the Pough-keepsie sunlight, I got a chance to appreciate her beauty, her radiance.

"Hyacinth, ah, what a remarkable woman. She still sends me a Christmas card every year without fail. She's the angel who settled our legal issues after Drew passed. It's expensive to die in America, don't you know Pop? You have to have all your affairs in order. We almost lost the house through such a nonsense of bureaucracy. God bless sweet Hyacinth. She came from a broken home, had few options – less than most even for the 1940s. Hyacinth though, well she had something a little extra, unbounded ambition for starters. She talked her future into existence whenever she came to visit us here that's for sure. *Miss Mary, I am going to be a lawyer,* she would say. This notion of hers was ridiculed by her own family, who would constantly say she needed to focus on being more like her brothers and sisters, and that she was getting ideas beyond her station. Once she broke free by running away from home, she began the process of elevating herself to where she felt she deserved to be. Hyacinth quickly found out she needed a lot more capital to exist, education is expensive, all the more so when you come from nothing. Soon enough she realised her options were slim and getting slimmer, and this led her to becoming a working girl. Hyacinth was a real looker and while sitting on a bench in Times Square was approached by a Broadway Madame as she scrolled through the small ads for jobs in the New York Times. This Madame told her she could make big bucks if she come work with her. Hyacinth declined the offer at first, yet setback after setback eventually meant she has no choice but to accept the Broadway Madame's invitation. This was strictly business, and she needed the money. This is how Drewford and Hyacinth's paths crossed."

Mary watched me react to this information awkwardly.

"NOT LIKE THAT POP," she roared with laughter, her giggle far larger than her petite frame. "Hyacinth worked three days a week, studied the other four. On the 'workdays' she would start late, her job was evening hours after all," Mary said this with another one of her cheeky winks. "On these days she would have her only meal of the day at Grand Central station. Her work took her out of town and the train was always her ride."

"And her meal?" I had to ask.

"A pastrami and pickle sandwich on rye bread with plenty of French mustard and a dollop of American mayonnaise. This was her favourite and that's what I made her whenever she came to visit us here. Hyacinth always went to a deli outside the station called 'Maud's delicatessen'. Maud looked out for Hyacinth and never once charged her. From the deli she would head to a quiet corner of the station. This quiet pastrami and rye corner was the same spot Drewford took his peaceful breaks, the place where he would eat his cheese and pickle sandwiches which he took to work each day in a brown paper bag.

"Drewford took his breaks at odd times of the day, but they some-how seemed to coincide with Hyacinth. They became friends and by the time Drewford died she was like a daughter to him, and he a father to her. She trusted Drewford completely. I know during those years whilst she was still getting her capital together, she kept a notebook, a list of events, who, where, everything and a lot more. It was a bit of security just in case the so-called shit hit the fan, pardon my French.

"She kept this sordid book in a locker at the station and as Hyacinth got to trust Drew more, she instructed him that if anything should ever happen to her, he must go to that locker and immediately send the book to a certain journalist at the New York Times. Real Marilyn Monroe conspiracy stuff. It would take another decade or so for the Broadway Madame to be busted by the cops. It was international news for weeks on end. This Madame's roots stretched as far as the White House, to chiefs of police, to the heads of movie studios and the bosses of the world's biggest businesses, criminal and legit. The lawyer instrumental in this epic downfall? That would be the lovely Miss Hyacinth, for as gorgeous as she was, she feasted on revenge, and later in life as she became a successful attorney of law one of her favourite things to do was plot revenge, cold, hot, mild, or spicy, sweet Hyacinth liked it all."

"Wild," I remarked.

"It really is. Miss Cynthia Andrews as she likes to go by these days is quite the formidable woman."

I almost spat out my tea, my mind instantly going into overdrive.

"Sorry what name was that, Mary?"

"Cynthia, Cynthia Andrews is what she goes by now," Mary repeated, completely unaware of the mind bomb that had gone off in my head.

It seemed like another lifetime ago but of course my old manager's name was also Cynthia Andrews. She was American. I was no mathematician, but I guessed the ages probably matched. I mean, surely it couldn't be the same Cynthia Andrews, could it?

I stopped Mary mid-sentence. I hadn't heard what she continued saying, the deductive reasoning running rampant in my mind had temporarily blocked out any other information coming in.

"Wait a second Mary. Did you say Cynthia Andrews?" I asked utterly startled.

Mary could tell my energy had changed and responded,

"What is it Pop? Have you heard of Hyacinth?"

"Heard of her? Mary, I think she was my manager. I knew her as Cynthia. We worked together for a number of years, right before the band got successful. We never talked much of her past life but we certainly got glimpses, she once told us that she had a 'wild come up,' and I remember her saying she left her family really young, and we always knew she was a big time lawyer in New York before retiring a very wealthy woman and moving to England. I guess once arriving in England she wasn't ready to put her feet up just yet, and decided the off the wall scene-change of managing a band would be her next adventure, and the moment when our stars aligned, and we crossed paths."

This jogged Mary's memory as she then confirmed that her 'Hyacinth' did indeed move to England after she retired, only to then un-retire to work in showbiz shortly after setting up shop in North London. What an unbelievable coincidence as once again I knew Cynthia lived in North London, she had this cool modern white building with lots of glass right on Hampstead Heath.

We both looked at each other in disbelief, we had been sitting here all this time with a mutual contact, not just any mutual contact the 'formidable' Miss Cynthia Andrews.

I asked Mary if she had an email address for Cynthia.

"Of course, Pop, I will DM you the info!"

"DM?" I blurted, shocked by her modern terminology. She didn't miss a beat.

"I'm old but not out of touch," she said with a mischievous smile whilst her slim olive-tanned arm pointed to the precious book resting on the table between us: a magical book lit by the sun like its own personal spotlight, reminding us why we are here. We both then spent an immeasurable amount of time staring silently at Drewford's book as if in a trance.

With Ellie hovering over us, photograph in hand, Mary finally broke our reverie.

"Would you like to put a face to these stories, Pop?" she asked.

"Oh my, yes ma'am," I said eagerly somehow adopting 1920s American etiquette.

Ellie handed me the antique bronze framed photograph and I saw the man himself smiling back at me.

Drewford, it seems, was as handsome as he was creative.

Along with his dynamite smile, Drewford had thick light hair parted to one side, big bright eyes, and a dashing moustache, clearly a very photogenic man.

I commented that I somehow recognised him.

As I looked at the photograph in wonder, Mary continued to talk about their life together. I enjoyed listening to her, just like Drewford she had a way with words.

It turns out when he retired in his late 60s, he would still go to the station three days a week to sit amongst the hustle and bustle that he had grown so used to.

One day Drewford didn't come back.

His colleagues found him sitting opposite one of the many

renowned artworks the station displayed on its walls. It seems he had been watching the world go by when, without any prior warning, his heart gave out and stopped beating. He had one of his note pads resting on his knee and a smile on his face.

"I never did see that notebook, perhaps that's it, Pop," Mary said pointing to the book.

The last page of Drewford's book did indeed have a detailed sketch of a high-ceilinged room with a large painting on the wall. The sketch had many people in it, some sitting on benches and some appearing to be heading somewhere else.

We speculated that this sketch of a painting in a crowd of people could be Grand Central Station. Perhaps this was Drewford's last living moment captured in his book. This emotional realisation was evident on Mary's face, her kind eyes instantly turning sad. Moments later Ellie came over to tell Mary it was time to take her medications and begin her daily stretching exercises. My afternoon with Mrs Alabama had flown by, and after near enough four hours of non-stop conversation it came to a close.

When we embraced for our final goodbye. I felt I had made a new friend.

The last thing she said to me before she disappeared into the house, "We don't do goodbyes Pop, just fond farewells."

She then passed me a brown paper bag with two cucumber sandwiches and a tangerine for the journey back to the city. Result.

Suddenly I noticed in my peripheral vision a large tortoise emerging slowly from under a growth of thick leafy shade near where we had been sitting all afternoon, the creature was heading towards a small orange water bowl by the front door.

Ellie clocked I'd noticed the tortoise and filled me in on the little prehistoric wonder's story.

"Lettuce was Mr Drewford's, apparently, he had him since he was a teenager. He loved him like a son. Lettuce is written into Miss Mary's will, in the event of her death a fund is to be set up to ensure Lettuce, who probably has a good decade or two left in him, will live them well. This will be my job," Ellie said while taking out a carrot from her apron. She presented it to senior Mr Lettuce in a very 'goo goo ga ga' manner. Lettuce's reaction was too slow to catch, but I am sure he was chuffed to bits.

So, with my packed snack safely stowed away in my class act of a briefcase, I re-applied my sunglasses and unfastened the top four buttons of my shirt. As I got to the end of Mary's street on my way to the station, I turned around to take one final look at the Alabama homestead. I could see Mary laughing with Ellie in the garden. As I continued to observe them, and their surroundings, I realised where I'd seen this postcard-like vision before. It was in Drewford Alabama's book – a sketch entitled HOME. The resemblance was uncanny.

It made me smile, a smile which didn't leave my face all day.

What a guy, what a lady, what an unforgettable day.

The train ride back from my Poughkeepsie pilgrimage had a different feel to it, knowing it was the same line Drewford once travelled gave the journey an extra special twist.

When we pulled up to Grand Central, I began walking around the place trying to imagine my every move from his perspective.

This was where Drewford spent a considerable amount of time. This was the place where he worked and potentially took direct inspiration for his own writings and drawings. This was where Drewford Alabama died.

You can't get more significant than that.

Grand Central is vast, my favourite part, like most people's is the main concourse. It's super cinematic and reeks of character, if you're in this glorious space you can't avoid the two sets of mountainous white marble stairs with their chunky brass handrails that lead up to a marbled viewing platform, a superb place to watch all comings and goings. As I stood there, I imagined Drewford standing in the exact same position, perhaps having his lunch, people watching, gathering ideas for stories or just keeping on top of his daily duties.

I couldn't help but appreciate the unbelievable acoustics of the place. I imagined a drum kit would sound monstrous there, like summoning Bonham for one last performance, a thunderous stairway to heaven.

To me there is no doubt about it, Grand Central Station is a very special place, its iconic status, just like Bonham's, fully warranted.

The day had been so amazing I'd completely forgotten about my evening's dinner arrangements. I'd managed to book myself a table at a newly opened restaurant in the Bronx that specialised in one meal, a meal close to my heart, and no, it's not pizza, but this culinary treat is one of those confused pizza foods I have mentioned before.

This place specialised solely in 26 different varieties of Mac and Cheese. The name: SMACK.

Later it would change to RETURN OF THE MAC.

Still equally questionable.

My appetite for life had returned, and with it my appetite for food. Food glorious food.

After exploring Grand Central Station twice over I was more than ready for my evening meal, I was stupidly ready, cutting to the chase. You could colour me giddy.

Leaving the station to fill my boots with *smack*, I passed a kiosk selling stationery, jewellery, and other miscellaneous New York City souvenirs. The man in charge of this mini island of hand crafted goodies also had a side hustle of drawing very impressive caricatures of tourists and celebrities. This mash up was clearly his shtick, I noticed he was currently working with a neon sharpie on an intricate drawing of the New York skyline with Michelle and Barack Obama flying hand in hand superhero-style in the sky. It sounds ridiculous, but you gotta trust me: it was really cool, loads of detail, bags of charm. This wasn't what initially caught my eye though.

What struck me was the various multicoloured notebooks displayed in the same way a magician would fan out a pack of cards. I'd filled my latest and left it in London, subsequently jotting down my thoughts digitally or on scraps of paper I found in my briefcase.

One of the greatest features on a smart phone is the notes section, but I, like Drewford Alabama have always found it very special to physically write words down. More thought, care and attention goes into it.

Just like when the vinyl finishes side A and you have to get out of your chair and walk over to the turn table to flip the record over before you can listen to the other side, to me that's marvellous. The extra effort required brings way more appreciation for the moment.

I was notepad-less which didn't feel great, something I planned to remedy right there and then. This was Drewford's station after all, perhaps a diary purchased from here would give me some extra magic, something I was always on the hunt for.

I zig zagged my way over to the compact island shop.

"Hey buddy, how much for the pink notebook and pen?"

The pen I was pointing to was half blue and half transparent, the top transparent side was filed with clear liquid and had a yellow New York city cab that floated up or down depending on the angle the pen was facing. It was irresistible.

"Eight bucks for you my friend," the man said with a New York accent.

"I will take two of each please, mate." I gave him twenty. "Keep the change."

As he passed me a bag containing my purchases, I wished him good luck and commented on his fabulous drawing talent.

As I walked off a young Asian couple asked him for a caricature sharpie doodle of themselves with their tiny fluffy dog. I couldn't help grinning when I saw the quirky artist begin to draw. I already knew the couple wouldn't be disappointed.

I was now suitably famished.

The thing is, when it comes to food heaven, the longer you wait, the better it is.

Think silky saucy molten cheese with small cubes of pancetta and succulent lobster buddying up brilliantly with perfectly al dente penne pasta and a mega frosty peach iced tea! What a place! An actual candle-lit restaurant just for macaroni and cheese. All this clever deliciousness had me thinking of the Poughkeepsie guy who invented Scrabble or the lady who invented the ice cream machine. I realised between cheesy mouthfuls of greatness that it always boils down to an idea.

Between further gluttonous mouthfuls I happily scribbled down every one of my musings, including this up-coming philosophical thought:

Never underestimate your ideas. You never know where they might take you.

I underlined this statement twice.

After *Smack* I headed back to my temporary Wall Street abode a very satisfied man. I was still processing the day. How could I not?

Mary and Drewford, their story, their life together, it had touched my heart deeply. I was *positively stirred*. I'd been so negatively stirred in my time to fully appreciate this moment.

The year – 2009 (Part 3)

The scene – Wall Street, New York.

Subject – Temporary Accommodation

Mood – Amused

On my last full day in the big city all I wanted to do was explore. I had my eyes set on visiting the Museum of Modern Art or 'MOMA' as it was known about town. I was told all the biggest and best artists featured there. All my faves: Dali, Haring, Pollock, Basquiat. It was the latter, Jean-Michel, who was featured on the Museum's illustrious walls that got me most excited as I was rather partial to his peculiar art.

I'd woken up well, my tummy still full from the evening's mac and cheese bonanza and my head still swirly from my time with Mary. I felt good, steady on my feet with my heart strong and only a slight hint of anxiety tickling the background of my thoughts. That day I would skip the rain box. From the sounds of it a couple were already clearly enjoying themselves in there. I wanted to leave them to it, certainly not be the one to go in after them. I hit Wall Street with a quickness, and oh what a transformation it was.

From my Bossa Nova bohemian hovel to the suited and booted running rampant on the financial golden mile. Wowza, the contrast was clear.

I stood out like a dishy sore thumb.

I love this area at night, but during the day…

"Please get me out of here."

That's exactly what I asked the lady driving the cab.

"You gotta tell me where sweetie, I can't read minds."

"Ah yes, my apologies. MOMA PLEASE."

The journey was quick and uneventful. I watched baseball on a tiny little screen fixed into the back of the driver's seat. I didn't have a clue what was going on, all I could see was multimillionaires trying to hit a ball with a stick. Most entertaining.

When I was in New York back in 1997, I said that I would never look at screens whilst in such modes of transport. I said something like, "looking out the window is always the best show in town." Well, I guess I'd learnt to appreciate what I once couldn't comprehend. I guess this was the old saying *never say never* having its contradictory way?

Speaking of comprehension, MOMA was closed.

Gutted.

Fortunately, all was not lost as directly opposite the Museum was the excellent Central Park.

I wandered over to explore the green expanse until I figured out what else to do with my day. The park was packed, the ice cream trucks had lines twenty deep. Rammowd!

It was early afternoon. It must have been summer holidays by the amount of parents begrudgingly towing themselves and their equally hot and bothered children around the park.

After a bit of exploring, I eventually found a place to hang out, my slice of sanctuary sitting on the massive prehistoric rocks that over-looked Central Park's watery expanse. The sheer precarious nature of my chosen spot made it the quietest place I could find. I sat with my legs hanging over the edge and listened back to the previous day's dictaphone recording of my conversation with Mary. Then I proceeded to be happily surprised when I procured a box of raisins I didn't know I had brought with me all the way from England inside the sneaky section of my class act of a briefcase. I massively over-estimated my cardigan's usefulness on this trip. It was far too hot for wool, instead I made great use of its cushion-like quality as a pillow.

The day was magnificent and I sat happily watching everything from the police horses patrolling the area with equine elegance, to the flash mob of elderly rollerbladers pulling spins and twirls with style and grace, it was a delight, and to add to this it was all set against the city's tall sky scrapers and foamy wispy white cirrus clouds moving with a snail-like pace in the gorgeous blue NYC sky.

I threw a few raisins to a lonely looking squirrel only to watch it run off in sheer disgust after inspecting my offering.

"Your loss," I said as I watched it disappear up a tree. My loss really, as those boxes are small and I was on the road to hungry, not there yet but the destination fast approaching.

I noticed Albee, as I nibbled on the last of my raisin treats.

I saluted him, "Hello mate, nice to see you over here!" At that very moment a pretty girl with short black hair and a green flouncy dress appeared out of nowhere. It seemed she witnessed me talking to a bird, I could see her laughing as she sat down a few Jurassic rocks away, once settled she looked over to me.

"Just trying to get away from…" She waved her hand towards the gaggle of screaming kids and equally screamy parents.

"I feel for you," I responded.

Her accent was different. I thought about it for a moment. I had to ask.

"Excuse me, what is that accent I hear? There's a few flavours going on. I can't put my finger on it."

She smiled cheerfully.

"I was born in Brazil, but I've lived in Sweden, Scotland, Japan and South Africa."

"That's what I would call Tutti Frutti," I responded.

"I like that. What does it mean?" she asked.

"It's a type of ice cream with lots of different flavours. It's delicious. It's the first thing I thought of. You're basically Tutti Frutti."

"Groovy," she responded with another marvellous smile and a double thumbs up.

Conscious that this had crossed the line from friendly conversation to *hitting on*, I thanked her for indulging my question and wished her a good day.

My derrière had gone numb from all the sitting on hard stone. I needed to get up and walk around, hunger had also fully reared its relentless demanding self. I threw on my shades and went about dusting myself off, all the while noticing in the corner of my eye that Tutti Frutti was watching me.

I liked it.

Even though she was way above my league, I enjoyed the attention.

It made me think of the time when I wouldn't have thought twice about a little subtle back and forth with a beautiful woman. Oh, how had times changed. At this point in life my confidence was like a complicated jigsaw, still putting itself together!

Lunch that day would be soup and salad from the Waldorf Astoria bar menu. Far beyond my current financial station in life I know, but fuck it, I deserved it. I once heard, *Every day you should treat yourself to something special. Don't plan or predict it, just let it happen.*

This was exactly that, and besides, I was drawn to the Waldorf. I walked from the park to the famous hotel without thought or hesitation, like a current in a river pulling me closer.

I was glad to go with it, as soon enough I was sipping one of the most appetising cream of mushroom soups I'd ever tasted. And how could I not? I splurged and ordered a world-famous Waldorf salad. When in Rome right?

Me being me, I took the complimentary warm bread rolls and discreetly filled them with cheese from the 35-dollar cheese board, making a fully improvised cheese sandwich which I proceeded to dip merrily into the soup.

"Maybe it's just me that subliminally wants all my food to be pizza," I thought.

If you give me some cheese and an edible vessel, I will always find a way to concoct a pizza substitute.

While paying my bill I saw something that instantly gave me butterflies.

The pretty girl from Central Park in the green flouncy dress was sitting at the bar at the opposite end of the opulent Waldorf Astoria dining room.

I waited a minute to see if she was with anyone, while brushing the crumbs of my T-shirt and with the tough corner of the napkin discreetly made sure I had nothing in my teeth. When I was confident she was like me and riding solo, I began the process of composing myself by counting backwards really slowly from ten with Buddha like control over my breathing. At zero I got up and walked over to the bar.

It was at this point that she took off her blue denim jacket and I clocked the shop label still attached to her dress.

Her dark brown hair nearly covered the offending tag. I had already scanned the room to see if anyone else saw it, no one had, she was certainly unaware as I watched her happily perusing the smart black leather cocktail menu.

As I approached, she noticed my presence and our eyes locked.

Seconds later I formally re introduced myself.

"Tutti Frutti, I must say it's a lovely surprise to see you again." I then discreetly whispered into her ear. "I thought you'd might like to know that your dresses price tag is hanging out."

"Oops!" was her twinkly eyed reaction, and in an impressive expertly swift motion she reached round and cleanly whipped it off.

As she put the offending tag into her compact black suede handbag, she turned to me as cool as a can be with fluttering eyes and dimples in her checks and said,

"Hello you."

She was comfortable in her own skin, owning the moment.

"May I join you?" I asked, "Comfier than Jurassic Park ain't it?"

With that bright smile, she gestured to the next tall bar stool along.

We ended up talking right through the afternoon, seldom stopping, one occasion was when Tutti scribbled onto one of the hotel's posh paper napkins. Once finished she folded it up neatly and placed it in her designer purse.

"All good thoughts must be written down," she announced.

"I couldn't agree more," I said opening up my briefcase then swiftly returning to the conversation brandishing my recently purchased notebook.

"I wrote this down last night," I said pointing to last night's double underlined notes about ideas.

"Never underestimate your ideas, you never know where they might take you."

"I am an ideas man," I proclaimed.

This is when she waved to the nearest bartender and ordered me a cup of 'English breakfast tea' and herself a Kir Royale with two cherries on a cocktail stick. Her presumptuous ordering made me laugh, before I could ask, she beat me to it with, "you don't look like a drinker". I laughed further. She didn't know the half of it,

I drank tea from fine china while she sipped on her Kir Royale. Both drinks were most fitting for such an ostentatious room.

During this libatious moment I noticed a small tattoo under her left forearm.

"What's the meaning?" I asked.

She aimed the tattoo text towards me so I could read it for myself.
"Time only moves forwards," I read out loud.

"Like the water in a stream," she added.

Tutti then showed me a tattoo under her right forearm. I was floored.

It was none other than a small blackbird tattooed almost to the inch where my small black bird is positioned, on exactly the same arm no less! I instantly showed her my own. Obviously, I didn't tell her about my 'spirit animal' Albee ... not yet.

We laughed and enjoyed the soaring coincidence. She then told me how her Grandparents, who she must have adored as she clutched her heart as she said the G word, would always call her 'little bird.' Tutti was indeed on the petite side.

When her drink arrived, she took the two skewered glacier cherries and bit the first with a very cute "Yum" she offered me the second which incited a very similar only slightly louder and what I hoped to be, 'cuter' "YUMMY" from me. This is when she excused herself to visit 'the powder room' at that moment I noticed her green summer dress was not only flouncy but speckled in tiny zebras with cherries balanced on their heads.

She was blissfully cool, cooler than a pack of peppermints. Right there and then I was smitten. That afternoon rolled on in a seren-dipitous daze, like we were the only two people in the whole of New York and for the first time ever my past melted away, and only the now mattered.

The now was feeling all kinds of special. That afternoon would be a permanently ingrained memory. I can still smell her perfume. I can still feel the air-conditioned chill in the room. I can hear the back-ground chatter, the shakes of cocktails being mixed and the clink and clank of cutlery on china. You really can't pick which life moments get this *never forget you* treatment but believe me I am so glad that this was one of them.

Eventually we talked ourselves out, a natural end to our afternoon. On her insistence we split the bill, and we got up to leave. As we walked out of the ritzy hotel looking like a hipster folk duo from the 60s, it struck me that we didn't even know each other's names.

I liked that.

Tutti Frutti was perfect and if I was totally honest, let's face it, realistic, I never really imagined I would see her again anyway. I already figured this would most likely just end up being a good memory. Those can be the best memories, with your imagination taking you to wherever you like. Ignorance is bliss and a good imagination can make it even more blissful.

Without much thought I blurted out, "Would you like to have dinner with me tonight?"

And without any hesitation whatsoever ever she responded with a big fat "NO."

"Oh, ok," I say trying not to sound disappointed. *Mmmmm that didn't work then did it Pop,* I thought painfully to myself. I was taken aback but not totally surprised, a good example of how living in your imagination can be a safer place at times.

What felt like minutes passed before a smile then appeared across Tutti's face accompanied with a belated, "Of course, I would love that."

She did this while reaching out to touch my hand as if she noticed my crest-fallen insecurity. My heart skipped a beat. Electricity.

"What do you fancy?" I asked gathering myself quickly.

"Fish and chips with plenty of HP."

She announced to the whole of Park Avenue throwing her arms in the air accompanied with a rock and roll mini scissor kick.

BLIMEY. She was incredible.

It would turn out that brown sauce ain't a thing in America. Their loss!

I can't even remember if it was a good chippie. The food was merely an excuse to spend more time together. Throughout the whole meal she was pouring salt on to the table arranging it with an upside-down wooden fork. I was so engrossed in our moment that I didn't notice she had been working on a salt drawing of me and her sitting on our separate Jurassic rocks from earlier.

It was remarkable – some talent!

The clean white salt against the bright yellow table really stood out, details and everything, extraordinary.

The next morning, I was leaving for England, we planned to meet up again for coffee and French toast drowned in maple syrup at a brasserie near her hotel in Tribeca called 'DeJour.'

As we talked and ate breakfast I presented her with a little gift.

"I have something for you, Tutti."

I gave her the spare notebook I bought in Grand Central Station and suggested, with a smile, that it was a better writing option than napkins.

On the first page I wrote:

> *Dear Tutti Frutti,*
> *Here's to chance encounters*
> *Central Park's Jurassic rocks and the Waldorf Astoria will*
> *never look the same again*
> *Next time we have fish and chips I will bring the HP*
> *Good vibes x*

We continued with our breakfast talking like we had known each other forever. I marvelled in her company. She was an absolute breath of fresh air. When time finally ran out, we reluctantly said our goodbyes. She told me that in a few months' time, 'work' would be bringing her to London.

"I would like to see you again," she said in a way that felt sweeter than ice cream as she confidently leant in to kiss me gently on my cheek.

"I would like that very much," I responded with my heart fully on my sleeve.

I will never forget how I left her pure gorgeousity sitting in the sunshine drinking her frothy latte. I swear we still didn't even know each other's names yet.

New York proved to be everything I'd hoped for…and so much more.

The word to sum it up precisely would be *EXCITED*.

(Diary extract)

I had no idea how much life needs excitement. It's only when you get a taste of it again after its absence do you realise how much you were missing it in the first place. I have been malnourished from the stuff!

These are the type of thoughts I was writing into my diary as I sat in the back of the golden yellow chariot taking me to the airport. I let fate decide whether I would stay or go. Or rather, I was letting Manhattan morning traffic decide if I should stay or go…that is a kinda fate I guess. Alas two hours later, me and fate took off from JFK. I looked out from my window seat and could see the sky dotted as far as the eye could see with Grandma's favourite clouds, the good old Strato Cumulus, like big fat fluffy cascading waves of weekend funfair cotton candy. That day they looked like they had been haphazardly thrown into the sky like a jumble sale patchwork throw.

I settled into the flight by reclining my chair ever so slowly hoping the lady sitting behind me wouldn't notice as I awkwardly ate into her space in uncomfortable increments. A drinks trolly visit later and I was eating complimentary dry roasted peanuts while sipping on some Moroccan whisky.

The scene was set. The soundtrack? My newly acquired rainforest compilation. As the plane hurtled through the sky, I felt particularly great. The greatest in years. I closed my eyes and nodded off. Good vibes. A very deep sleep ensued, and subsequently flying somewhere over the Atlantic Ocean I dreamt that I was on a fast-moving train. This train wasn't anything like the one to Poughkeepsie, this was one of those old diner trains with lots of rows of elegantly decorated candle lit dinner tables.

It was nighttime and the train was speeding towards its destination of I don't know where. A few other groups and couples sat at tables around us eating very well put together food. Everyone in the carriage was deep in conversation, yet all the chatter was completely drowned out by the big old steam engine powering the locomotive train. Mary and Drewford were my co-stars to this dream. We were sitting together at one of the elegant dining tables with the two of them opposite me. I remember as clear as day the effects of the warm candle lit glow giving them both a look of full-on vibrancy, a look only truly achievable through youth and good genes. They were both in their early thirties. Mary wasn't called Mary anymore though, she was going by the rather unusual name of Wolfie Pigman. I instinctively knew this already.

Wolfie was tipsy from the free-flowing champagne. She was literally 'bubbly.' We were all having a riotous time. Wolfie was the youngest record executive to ever head up a major record label, a star in her field.

Once again, I already knew this.

Drewford, like Mary, was no longer Drewford. He was known as Vincent.

Vincent DeVille.

Vincent was a big-time record producer slash celebrity.

I knew his work and I was intimidated by his success. He was aloof and very much the ying to Wolfie's yang with his impossibly cool, scruffed-up hair and avocado tinted sunglasses. He was without a doubt, quite a presence.

We were eating ragù served by waiters wearing white gloves and pencil thin moustaches. We shared warm fresh rolls by breaking them into pieces and passing them around, the true meaning of 'breaking bread.'

In this dream I was an artist, and Wolfie the hot shot label exec was making every effort to woo me. I was playing coy, but secretly loving every second of it. Wolfie had been desperate to meet me for a long time. I guess I had been happy to oblige as long as it was on a train. She brought along her colleague Vincent as she thought we would hit it off, perhaps thinking we could work together on making an album. Vincent, who liked to be called *Vincenzo*, spoke only twice throughout the whole dreamy vision. When he did, Wolfie and myself were poised in anticipation of his every word.

His gravely raspy voice was full of character. I imagined he smoked lots of cigarettes and gargled bourbon for breakfast. It transpired Vincent had a concept which he was very excited about, his idea,

"We should have lots of different singers on the album, each song a different singer."

"Like a kaleidoscopic of voice and sound!"

"You gotta call it the Life and Times of Drewford Alabama, man!"

Wolfie nodded her head in complete agreement, and I was suitably intrigued.

At this moment in the dream, I recall looking at the reflection of myself in the thick glass window of the train.

I was more than intrigued. I was beaming ear to ear.

"LET'S DO IT!" I announced, raising my champagne glass full of chocolate milk. Wolfie clocked our different drinks. In response she said, "We heard you don't drink now, good for you!"

The second we clinked our crystal cups together I came back to reality.

The typical Pop Morrison occurrence of waking up with an airplane steward leaning over me practically shaking me awake is a bit of a theme, I guess.

"Please adjust your seat and pull up the blind in preparation for landing, sir."

"Yep, sure thing," I croaked, my voice still half asleep.

I cleared my throat and threw a chewing gum into my mouth (a long haul flying essential.)

My dream was broken abruptly, but enough was firmly set for me to write down in my new Grand Central notebook. I scribbled as quickly as possible trying hard to keep up with my inspired mind, slightly fearful I would forget a crucial thought or memory.

With my New York novelty pen flaming hot from its high intensity workout, I sat both pad and pen on my lap and placed the tiny aeroplane pillow on top of them both, as if instinctively protective of the words I'd just written.

This was not like any Drewford Alabama dream I'd previously had, as this time round I knew exactly what to do. My head was alight with thoughts, like a fireworks night in my mind, every passing moment a beautiful idea taking off in a colourful explosion. It was decided.

I was going to be my own band and I was going to make my own album.

I now knew exactly what to do, thoroughly inspired by my sky-high dream. My immediate plan of action was to use Drewford Alabama's book of words and sketches as inspiration to write songs. I would do exactly what Vincenzo said and get a different singer to feature on each track.

What were his words again?

Like a kaleidoscopic of voice and sound man!

I thought, "That works for me!"

When I got back home, I picked up my guitar and tape recorder. Over the next few weeks everything flowed effortlessly, it was like a dam had burst open and endless musical ideas poured out of me. It wasn't long until I'd amassed a great wealth of incredible music.

I was really doing it. I was making an album inspired by Drewford Alabama's book.

I was going to tell Drewford's stories for him. I would bring his work into the world in a way he couldn't and in doing so I could feel it revitalising my creative spirit, a total overhaul, something I had needed for a very long time. My dream epiphany plan of action written inside my new Grand Central Station notepad went a little like this.

Pop, invite a singer over to the studio, flick through the pages of Drewford's book until a sketch, story, line or phrase is found that suitably inspires then turn it into song. Be your own band.
− Flight BA 457, Seat 9a, NYC to London − 25 July

That was the plan, and I was sticking to it. Every day I went about pouring my heart into melody, whereas before I worked with beats, now I had opened a whole new world for myself, born out of not having a guitar player and singer to work with. I became my own guitar player, and vocalist. I wasn't the best at either, but it was more than enough to express myself. I even thought my voice had character, not like a classic singer, more like odd but recognisable. I wasn't thinking about that though. I was sticking with the dream, with what Vincenzo said: a different singer on each song.

I loved this idea and went about putting together the music for twelve pieces I hoped to turn into songs. I was initially worried I would find it difficult to get artists to collaborate with, but it turned out I had some unexpected love out there on these musical streets. I wrote a list of people I wanted to work with and found them online. To my great surprise almost each and every one of them said yes. Emma's Imagination was the first artist I contacted, and within the hour I received the reply to my message, "I AM IN." When almost every other artist responded in a similar happy snappy way my energy couldn't be contained. I had my squad, Emma's Imagination, Fyfe Dangerfield, Willis, Bnann, CA Smith, The Lost Brothers, Chali B, Dawn Landes, Patrick Walden, Josh Weller and Sam Semple.

With that, I was off. It was all planned and arranged quickly and when each artist arrived at the studio, the first order of the day would be tea and biscuits, this was mandatory and an integral part of the creative process. Once suitably refreshed I would go about explaining the great story of Drewford Alabama leading up to the ultimate revelation of his intriguing book.

I would then start to play the music I'd been working on, and after a few minutes something would always *just click* and my singing friend would respond with…

"Got a microphone?" or "Lets record!"

When the vibe hits, you gotta move, and to great delight every time I pressed record a beautiful voice would fill the cosy, dimly lit studio, and in real time I saw my idea inspired by a dream come to life.

The album was no small task and would take a number of years to finish, but once complete it became very apparent that with the help of my special guests, and of course, the great Drewford Alabama we had made a very special record. We had the title already. Vincenzo gave it to me in that dream: *The Life & Times of Drewford Alabama.*

The year – 2011

Location – Denmark Street

Mood – Deductive

I thought perhaps my dream on the plane from New York was what all the previous dreams were leading up to. I thought the making of The Life & Times of Drewford Alabama album was the point to it all. I thought wrong.

I realised when I invited a radio DJ friend of mine, Abraham Wallace, to the studio whilst I was still making the record. Wallace lived nearby and had joined my running group. Subsequently we became friends and one Sunday lunch over a cheat day Pizza Pie, I told Wallace all about Drewford Alabama. He was so intrigued he came to the studio after our pie and insisted I played him the music which he completely fell in love with.

When I finally released the album Wallace invited me on his evening radio show to talk about Drewford and play some tracks, I couldn't say no could I? When the vibe is there you gotta jump right?

Speaking on Wallace's show was the first time I'd ever been so candid about finding the book. It was also the first time I'd ever even hinted at discussing the dreams and everything else that was wrapped up along with it. It was a poignant perspective grabbing moment if ever there was one, one that brought to light a colossal aspect of my story that still remained unanswered.

While walking home from the station it dawned on me that during this whole reinvigorating period I hadn't once thought about those mystery riddled dreams. In fact, as soon as I returned home from that epiphany inducing NYC trip, all Drewford Alabama related dreams stopped. Nothing strange about that really. I was back to dreaming about rainbows and sunbeams, which I only took to mean that all the previous dreams' messages and meanings had been received.

Relieved at finding my once lost inner joy, I had dismissed those cryptic messages that were such a big part of my recurring nighttime visions.

What am I saying? The biggest part!

Clearly, I had unfinished business, and with this running through my mind I picked up my pace as I headed back home. A tremendous thought had struck me, one of those eureka moments had occurred.

Upon arrival at Casa Del Pop, I immediately actioned my plan by collecting every scribbled down Drewford Alabama related dream. It was time to reconnect with every one of them. Locating everything Drewford was easy. I'd decided there was no better place to store all my Drewford material than within my flame scorched sweetie tin. After all, it had survived an almighty fire. Because of this, I considered it lucky and more than worthy of containing such important artefacts.

I kept the tin hidden behind my vinyl record collection in the corner of the Denmark Street flat. I hid the tin and its contents like it was a pot of gold. It was as valuable as gold to me; it deserved to be treated in the same manner.

Once I retrieved my lucky tin, I pushed aside an ongoing, heated game of Scrabble sitting on the reclaimed-wood kitchen table. With all the priceless scraps laid out in front of me, an almighty rush of emotion hit like a rogue wave catching you off guard while you're happily frolicking in the ocean.

The evening was stirring in that way. I wasn't afraid of the emotional waves; I was surfing them.

First things first I put the kettle on. Nothing adds to clarity more than a cup of steaming hot Moroccan whisky.

My eureka moment?

Well, it seems obvious now but I was going to write down all the variations of my Drewford Alabama dream on one piece of paper. There were seven of them in total written on scraps of paper, napkins, even a menu for the Rising Dragon – a nice Chinese restaurant on Chancery Lane. It made more sense for them to all be in one definitive place. This was the logical prelude to clarity. After a few sips and the tiniest amount of procrastination, I began to scribble.

Once I finished compiling the dreams, I sat there staring at them as if this act of organising everything into one place would be enough to solve the riddle.

I knew these words and letters were more than just random dreams or abstractions. They were meaningful, after all, why would they have kept appearing if there wasn't something deeper trying to be said within them?

I was completely engrossed yet it was late and after a brief period of going round and round I didn't reach a conclusion. My eyes got tired and frustration was creeping in which annoyed me. I needed to pick it up. This was important! Somehow I knew tonight was the night the reign of mystery surrounding my riddle filled dreamy messages was coming to an end.

I needed a break, that's all it was, at this very moment the old dusty grandfather clock that came with the flat began its unmelodious dissonant chime. It was midnight, which got me thinking about one of Drewford Alabama's written musings,

With time comes perspective.

What I needed was the latter, Drewford believed they both go hand in hand. Why not!

I decided to go for a walk and get some 'time' away from my cryptic scribbles and hopefully gain some much-needed perspective.

I stealthily left the flat closing the front door in the most silent covert manner I could muster. As I flicked the light on in the communal stairway the bulb sizzled and, in a flash, died a sudden death. It did this every few weeks, I was used to it.

I held the handrail tightly as I carefully manoeuvred myself down the three flights of stairs towards street level. Firm on my feet, I buzzed myself out of the building and instantly felt refreshed in the cool night air. I made my way through a deserted Denmark Street heading towards Charing Cross Road where I entered a narrow alleyway to Soho.

I always hated going down this alleyway. The folk who left the clubs at the end of the night on weekends always seemed to use it as their own private *en suite* bathroom. That night I held my breath as the noxious dehydrated piss stench was ripe. I cleared the rancid alley in record time. Only then could I begin my peaceful perspective-inducing walk.

Soho is a great place to stroll, the old intertwining streets and history drenched buildings are an amazing source of inspiration. I walked down an empty Greek Street into Soho Square and watched the trees sway in the breeze of Soho's only grassy area. The golden streetlamps against the oak trees created moving shadows from the leaves and branches bouncing off the buildings, it looked like a creepy cartoon. This charming, spooky sight entertained me, and I stopped to watch for a few minutes before continuing on my way.

There are many directions you can take from Soho Square. I chose Frith Street as I have fond memories of the bars and restaurants, I used to play all those years ago when I was a fresh faced up and coming musician. I could have chosen Greek Street, but I didn't fancy passing OAK, my old workplace. I hadn't been on that street since the day I found out Grandma was dying. Tonight wasn't the night.

As I started walking down jazzy Frith Street, the clarity I was looking for to accompany my eureka moment hit me, and inspiration filled my head like a thousand Christmas lights being turned on.

I swiftly headed home.

After navigating the precarious pitch-black staircase, I re-entered my flat, tip toeing like a ninja on a mission to pen and paper.

I looked at my previous deductive methods from a completely different angle.

My most recent inspiration had led me to re-write every dream as if it was a paragraph of dialogue in the order of its appearance.

I wrote in my very best all-capital writing. I was so focused on my legible scribble I didn't even acknowledge what I was jotting down. When I finished, I whispered back to myself in amazement at what I had just written.

HELLO ANDREW, YOU FOUND ME. TIME IS ON YOUR SIDE. DON'T FORGET. THE MIDDLE IS FOR YOU. THE END.

I instinctively underlined the words that intrigued me the most.

The middle is for you…

Hmmm.

The middle is for me, is it?

I didn't dwell and continued with my inspired train of thought, YOU FOUND ME stood out.

"What did I find?" I said out loud.

THE BOOK! I immediately responded enthusiastically to myself.

I flicked through the pages looking for something to make sense of my detective work, and within moments I reached the middle of Drewford's tatty book. I was most surprised to see it was completely blank – oddly blank considering every other page was crammed full.

It was strange. Why would just one page in the middle of the brimming book be empty, and seriously, how the hell did I previously miss this?

Eyes wide shut!

I knew there and then I had just cracked a small part of my puzzle, I was on a roll. And then it struck me. Why not repeat my same deductive method with the cryptic letters?

This time instead of pen and paper I took the wooden letters from the heated Scrabble game and arranged the pieces in the order of when they first visited me.

I was astounded, the whole moment was surreal, tantalising even.

"Y O U H A V E O N E W I S H"

"You have one wish," I said repeatedly out loud while pacing around the room.

I did this until my loud musings woke up my slumbering wife next door.

WIFE!

Did he just say wife?

I know, I know.

My apologies for not mentioning it before, but I wanted to surprise you.

SURPRISE!

I married Tutti Frutti!

She came to London as planned and our relationship blossomed quickly from playful courting right the way into a full-on love. We were joined at the hip within the month, Bonnie and Clyde style, minus the bank robbing.

Our first proper date was in London watching Nick Cave at the Royal Albert Hall.

We had the cheapest tickets standing all the way at the top balcony, the furthest you could possibly be. It was so far in fact that Nick Cave and his musicians looked like mere ants scuttering around the iconic stage.

It sounded glorious, the most excellent soundtrack to such a special night. We couldn't keep our hands off each other. We were like two cats in a bag or as Tutti herself recently commented, "We were like a giggling pack of hyenas in a butcher's shop."

That was exactly how it was going. Well, that is, until we could both sense that other people around our loved-up bubble wanted us to leave, and leave we did, getting out just before the end of the show.

The West London night air was a balmy bliss. There was no way we were going to do anything other than enjoy it a bit more. We just walked and talked, holding hands, planning our future together, for now we were inexplicably twinned. There was no official announcement, no debate, question, or request, it was just so, the way it was supposed to be and has been ever since.

I popped the question whilst we were sitting on a Ferris wheel at the Christmas winter wonderland in Hyde Park. We loved the winter wonderland. I'd just won Tutti a heart shaped pillow from a cork shooting rifle, I'd knocked down a trio of tin cans and as a prize she picked out the soft pink heart. When we headed to the Ferris wheel I started preparing to ask the big question. I took the jelly ring from a sweetie bag we bought from an old time sweet stall at the entrance to the fun and games area. I only bought the bag of sweets because I could see a temporary wedding band could be fashioned from one of the ring-shaped jelly gum sweeties.

I had been looking for the right moment to ask for Tutti's hand in marriage. I'd been racking my brains for months about how I was going to pop the big one.

I thought about a balloon ride over the English countryside, a boat ride down the Thames, I even thought about having a personal message read out by the DJ on her favourite morning radio station.

Instead, I improvised.

She looked so beautiful under the colourful fairground rides that for some reason I just felt this was the moment to *pop* the question.

So, Pop 'popped' and as her smile said YES, my elated eyes turned to saucers, and we be both fell into each other laughing. We then kissed and held each other tightly as we looked out across London from the top of the flashy amusement park ride.

I could see my old room at Benjy's Dad's posh Park Lane hotel in the distance, I had come a long way since then. I understood that Park

Lane life was merely a few pages in the grand scheme of my life's book, a book which I was now back in full control of writing. What's more, I couldn't have been more excited to be embarking on a new chapter with my best friend, my wife, Tutti Frutti Morrison. *CONTENT* is the word.

Any previous feelings of love and longing were blown out of the water with Tutti.

This was the real deal, the type of love that films or books and plays are about.

We got married in a Scottish Castle on fireworks night, most appropriate for a fairytale love like ours. Tutti says we married on the fifth of November so I would never forget the date, the old saying 'remember, remember the fifth of November' rings true, although the real reason is because of how much she loves fireworks. In our loved-up mind, having a fireworks display marking the historic occasion on every anniversary is just for us!

The year – 2011 (continued)

Location – Denmark Street

Time – Dead of Night

Mood – Solving Mysteries and Alphabetical Riddles

With Tutti now awake, we picked up an old conversation about painting the ceiling of the flat powder pink or olive green. Whilst debating, I made her favourite night time beverage: warmed chocolate-flavoured oat milk. It sent her right back to sleep, right after we decided on pink that is.

With her tucked into bed I went back to my detective work with gusto.

I had YOU HAVE ONE WISH spelt out in small Scrabble pieces on the kitchen table, the moment screamed pure and utter intrigue. Instinctively I stepped away from the kitchen making sure I kept a firm eye on the message spelt out on the table. I thought for a second that perhaps I was dreaming, and the letters would fly away and turn into unicorns or some similar fantastical thing.

With all this going on in my mind I opened the doors to the terrace to let some cool summer night air into the room. This woke Roscoe who got up, looked at me adorably with his smiley round eyes, did a huge yawn, followed by a massive stretch, then headed out to his wooden kennel by the orchid dome. I watched him while I unwrapped a strawberry lolly that Dr Grace gave me, which I found in my jacket pocket. You're never too old to turn down a free sweet.

As the artificial strawberry flavours took over my taste buds, I thought was this really happening? It was all a bit crazy. Was I going completely batshit insane, or what?

I deduced that my dreams had been cryptically trying to tell me that I had one wish and the blank page in the middle of Drewford's book was the place I should write it.

'I am tripping,' I thought, laughing quietly to myself.

Perhaps I was high, I knew I wasn't, hadn't been in years. I thought I must be sleeping, and this was another one of my wild dreams, but once again I knew this wasn't the case.

Eventually I joined Roscoe on the terrace, get some air, think it through a little.

And here I began to toy with the idea of *what if I did have one wish to make?*

The '*what if*' running around round and round in my mind.

Just what if?

I looked up to the stars and tried to comprehend what single wish I would make if all of this was actually true.

I looked at the bright moon and began to talk to it like a dear friend. "What do you think buddy, am I going mad?"

I remember I was half expecting a shooting star or some additional random act of bizarreness, but of course nothing appeared, just a couple of kids on the street below smashing a bottle causing a ruckus, and my feathered friend Albee balancing on top of a ledge on the building opposite Mr Kinsey's.

Eventually I decided I would have another look in the morning, a fresh perspective and all that. I picked up Roscoe and headed back inside closing the doors and the big city behind us. I put some food out for the boy and began my '*getting ready for bed*' routine. While I was brushing my teeth, I looked at myself in the mirror and thought, FUCK IT!

I knew exactly what my wish would be the second I entertained the thought.

Then I walked over to the kitchen table and with foamy toothpaste dribbling down the corner of my mouth, I wrote the wish into the blank middle page of Drewford's book.

There was only one thing I wanted so I wrote it down in the middle page without any hesitation punctuation or grammar.

I really wish I was in an amazing band...

I closed the book with a smirky expression across my face and placed it back into the flame scorched tin with the rest of my Drewford Alabama artefacts.

That wish was the one thing I missed the most in the whole world.

I hadn't felt the same in my professional life since it had gone.

I had never felt truly content without the camaraderie of a proper band around me.

I laughed at myself for thinking that any of this could be real but like I said, fuck it. That night I lay in bed reliving my evening's detective work. I recounted the timeline. It had been exactly ten years since I first discovered Drewford's book. A whole decade. What a journey, what a ride, and with these memories flying round my head my eyelids got heavy and I drifted off to sleep. I couldn't have known, but that night I would have my last Drewford Alabama related dream.

I was in Grand Central Station. I instantly recognised its iconic architecture. I knew I had definite purpose being there, like an important appointment or something. I walked around taking in the familiar sights and busy sounds. I stopped for a moment and watched the second hand slowly move around the four-sided antique clock sitting squat above the information booth in the main concourse. The clock's hands gliding smoothly over the clock face reminded me of a ballerina floating effortlessly across a stage. The time was 5.15, which explained the station's intense bustle. I carried on exploring and avoiding the heaving throngs where possible until a clearing of busy travellers opened up ahead of me. It was as if everything in front of me melted away leaving only a man sitting on a bench up in the distance. He was very recognisable, frustratingly so!

It took me a moment to work it out who he was, so I moved around the station keeping a firm eye on him. It wasn't connecting, but I knew I had seen this chap before, and as I moved closer, I racked my brains further until something clicked in place and I realised who he was.

I gasped. It was none other than Mr Drewford Alabama in all his reverential magnificence. With this realisation I immediately made my way over to him with the clear intention of saying hello. As I got close enough, I could see him working on a drawing on the open note pad resting on his knee. I recognised it from the book I discovered, a sketch of the artwork painted on the wall in front of him.

Poignantly this is the same sketch Mary and I suspected he was drawing during the last moments of his life. I got closer and without looking up Drewford spoke to me in a deep oaky voice as if he knew I was right there standing over him.

"I have been waiting for you, Andrew. Come sit here."

He gestured to the next seat along, pencil in hand.

I sat down. He looked at me straight on and I saw his face close up. He was Grandpa age, with bright eyes and a welcoming smile, as handsome as the picture Mary showed me in their Alabaster rose-scented garden.

"You know I got real worried for a few moments there," he announced in his oaky voice, rubbing his old soft hands together as he spoke. I noticed he was wearing exactly the same ruby wedding ring as Mary.

Matching wedding rings. "Of course!" I muttered to myself.

"You've been on a hell of a ride, you almost didn't make it, you even came close to giving up, didn't you?"

I was trying to play catch up with every word Drewford spoke, as if I was late to a conversation that had already long since begun. Instead of getting anxious or flustered I sat there in awe listening to him speak. I trusted the moment and I knew it was time to listen. I suspect he'd been waiting to say this for a very long time. I wanted to respect his words in silence. Besides, every sentence he spoke became more gripping than the last.

"You see, Andrew, you didn't find my book by accident. It was fate, and fate is akin to luck which can be gently nudged here and there to work out in different ways. When I first saw you, I knew there was something a little extra going on, something that only comes around every once in a while. I had that very same 'vibe' as you would call it, and in a different era and circumstance, perhaps I would have been able to take that 'vibe' and do what you did."

At this point I couldn't help interjecting.

"What did I do, Drewford?"

"You followed your dreams, Andrew! When you first discovered drums, you followed your heart and inner instinct right through until... Well, you know when, don't you?"

I nodded my head slowly in pained acknowledgment.

"Andrew, I knew when I first saw you that you would need me, and you know what, I also needed you."

I wanted to stop him there and then, to ask why he could have possibly needed me, but his words had now begun to have a gentle authority to them.

"Those recurring dreams you had when you relive that moment you discovered my book, the disappearing ink and invisible handwritten messages. They were all me."

I couldn't hold it in, I had to stop him.

"Drewford if you wanted to tell me something why didn't you just write it as is? Why so cryptic. I don't mean to question your ways, but wouldn't that have been far easier?"

"I knew you would ask this question," he responded looking away with a sigh. "I would have loved to tell you every single thing you needed to know. You were simply not ready, you needed to go through all those trials and tribulations life threw at you to learn how to truly value what you had, what you have now, and what you will have later, all that pain you went through taught you something didn't it? You needed to experience everything you have been through so you could earn the tools you will need to go forwards. To be frank, you wouldn't have survived without learning those life lessons. You're a sensitive soul just like me, which I recognised immediately."

"I am sorry Drewford, but I have to ask. What's going on here? Who exactly are you?"

"Believe it or not Andrew...Oh I am sorry. That's not your name is it! You're still registered up here as Andrew you see. Let me start again, but before I do, please call me Drew, we are old friends now.

"Believe it or not Mr Pop Morrison, I am an angel. There's a few types of angel and I am of the guardian variety. The most important of all angels if I do say so myself. I know it's hard to believe in your world these days Pop, but that's exactly what I am."

It surprised me too.

"I have held this position ever since I kicked the bucket 30 years, 57 days, 16 hours, 12 minutes and four seconds ago. Another hard to fathom truth which I shouldn't really share with you, but because it pertains to questions, I know you will want to ask, I shall anyway ... When you die Pop Morrison, you will also most likely become an angel too. Only the people with pure empathetic hearts and open imaginations can become one. This is partly why we can communicate.

"What we have is very special, extra special in fact, it's not typical and only happens when an angel and *guardee* share such a deep routed connection like we most certainly do. Cases like ours Pop are very rare.

I believe the last known case of a similar angelic and human synergy happened in 1979 with a little Alaskan girl named Elky. An angel's job has echoed through time with the most important duties – keeping people like yourself pure. Sadly, these days fewer angels appear every year, and I hate to say it, but there will probably be a time when there won't be any more of us left. The official cause of death? People stopped believing! We try to avoid talks of this nature though Pop, positivity is a powerful force as you know all too well."

Clearly Drewford could see the fathom building in my awkward facial expressions, incomprehension was screaming from my wide-eyed appearance. The saying a deer in the headlights comes to mind!

"I imagine it's a lot to take in but please let me educate you a little in our angel ways. Angels have powerful instincts, we can see into the distance, but not the immediate future, this ability is worth mentioning as it's essential in aiding an angel on their journey to becoming a guardian."

At this moment I pinched myself. I had to, right?

It was all so hard to believe, yet it was as real as the pain in my pinched forearm.

I went with it, I was hardly going to object, this was after all, the main man himself.

Drewford continued.

"I have been watching over you since the day you walked past your school music block. The day you came face to face with your rhythmic destiny is the day our journey together began. Even then I could see what your life would become, and I knew you would need my assistance further down the road. It's the human trait of unpredictability which got in our way," he said with a solo chuckle. "Here's the thing Pop, an angel's job is only complete when the person chosen to watch over is deemed to be living with a pure heart and positive intentions or as you would say, with 'good vibes.' It's easy to start with this spirit, but to carry on throughout life with these vibey ways can be a very hard prospect to achieve.

"It's imperative that characters like you keep their natural sense of wonderment and pure hearted empathetic inclinations. Keeping these intact throughout whatever life throws at you is essentially a guardian angel's sole focus. If this job is successful and both guardian and *guardee* succeed in maintaining these gifts then an angel's job is done.

"An angel can see into the distant future, and thus once the precious character commodity of 'pure vibes' is no longer in jeopardy the best part about being an angel is made available. Now if you thought an angel was a hard to comprehend concept, an angel's parting gift will add a further lack of understanding to the mix. I must admit it was hard for me to fathom when I was first told. With success an angel's parting gift is the ability to grant one single wish. This deal of giving and receiving a wish dates back to the beginning of time and features on the first page of the handbook '*the laws of life and after life living*,' a book which is presented to you when you first join the league of angels. It's worth noting a bit of angelic legislation in the small print that the very moment a wish is granted there is a 32-and-a-half-day period of time where it can be revoked at any point. If said wish is squandered or lessons unlearned it's taken back without hesitation. 'I want to be a billionaire or the president of the United States of America,' for example, would both be revocable examples. Are you keeping up Pop? I know it's a lot to take in."

"I believe I am, Drewford,' I responded.

I proceeded to list each step in a bid to show I was keeping up with these frankly hard to comprehend concepts.

Step one: Choose someone with angelic tendencies to watch over.
Step two: Assist in keeping said angelic tendencies intact.
Step three: Grant wish.
Is there a Step 4?

"There is Pop, but in the way all previous steps aid the human being in the land of the living, the fourth step is reserved for the angel in the form of a reward. An angel's reward is based solely on the success of the *guardee*. It's a frightful task, for if it all goes wrong and your *guardee* loses their sense of wonder, or if the wish is ultimately wasted, an angel's fate is sealed by being permanently stuck in afterlife limbo until the end of time."

Drewford saw my eyes begin to widen.

"Stay with me Pop, it goes like this. Wherever you may be when you eventually pass away, wherever your last breath is taken or last heartbeat beats is where you get stuck. It's not called 'after life limbo' for nothing. For me it was this place," he says waving his arm across Grand Central Station like a fisherman casting their line to water. Drew continued,

"We all know of those haunting stories of places where people passed on, where a guardian angel backed the wrong horse and was unable to steer their subject back on track, ultimately losing the only chance of fully passing on to the other side. I hear stories about the angels who get stuck, it's not a pretty situation Pop. This is why spooky ghost stories are not happy stories. Let's just say those things that go bump in the night, were once angels who are now stuck forever roaming bitterly, causing havoc and fright. It must be noted that not everyone becomes an angel, and it's also worth adding it's not everyone's cup of tea to have such an important after-life role. I understand the quandary, you've lived your life and before you get to move on fully you have to watch over someone for potentially a really long time. Most just want to pass on through to the other side and that's exactly what happens.

"Speaking from experience, when I first arrived on the angelic scene, I was given the choice to opt out – an option I almost ran with. You have to understand Pop, I was furious! My death was totally unexpected. I had no idea when I first sat here all those years ago that I would never be going home to my Mary.

"Until then I always thought everything in life was, I guess, pre-set, like a set of dominos falling one after the other, I believed all you achieve and all you experience was set in stone for every single one of us. Pop, I was so wrong. There's so much more going on than you could possibly imagine. It's beyond rhyme or reason, fantasy or fable. The moment I died everything changed, it wasn't the end though, far from it. Upon arrival I was informed by the most glorious all-encompassing light what my options were. There was no voice, no white bearded man or ethereal maiden, the information was just within me the very moment the glorious glow engulfed me. From then on, I knew what my role as an angel entailed. What was important, I knew one of the rewards for doing a good job would be getting to pick whoever I like, mutually speaking that is, to spend afterlife eternity with. Well, of course when I learnt that information there was no question about what I should do. It was the long, potentially more perilous road, but being able to spend the rest of eternity with my Mary was all I needed to know. I also knew without a shadow of doubt the option of 'passing on to the other side' was a no-no. Never has anyone come back from that place to describe what it's like. Perhaps it's a big old party, or perhaps there's nothing, zero, zilch, nadda, the true meaning of 'the end'. I couldn't risk not seeing Mary again. Being an angel would pose its own challenges, but the possibility of being reunited with her when her time was up, gave me all the incentive I could ever need.

"I took my new angelic role very seriously, I studied my handbook page by page, hundreds if not thousands of times. I would leave no stone unturned, learn everything I possibly could to maximise my chances of being a successful angel. I missed Mary so desperately. The thought of being able to spend eternity with her would just about make up for my abrupt departure. Of course, this could have resulted in me turning into a ghost, but there was no doubt that this was a risk worth taking. All my studies brought me to the conclusion that picking the right person to watch over should be done with great care and foresight, and using the angelic training provided combined with my natural beatific instincts I eventually found you.

"I saw that glint in your eye when you got your first taste for drums, it was the sparkle I had faith in, that look was undeniable. So that was it, just like that, I was your guardian angel, and from that point on I have done exactly what the job title describes. In times of unpredictability, I couldn't do more than give you little hints, clues, glimpses, nudges, shakes, pushes and pulls, all minor stuff, sometimes even the occasional visit here and there. Like I say, minor. In many ways an angel's forte is planting subliminal seeds of ideas. Sometimes seconds, minutes, days, months or even years in advance. We are also masters of misdirection, *déjà vu*, coincidence, and luck, yep, luck!

"Your bag on that New York trip wasn't lost by accident! You see I knew all too well that if I could get you to the city bagless you would visit that thrift store all your friends had told you about. I knew, with your eccentric style choices, there was no way you wouldn't want that tartan suitcase with fetching salmon pink lining to replace the one I lost for you.

"Once you bought that it was only a matter of time until you discovered my book. I must say you surprised me in how quickly you managed to find it. I was most impressed. As time went by and your life unravelled something happened with me. I began to understand and value what a noble and privileged duty being an angel actually is, and how important it is in keeping a harmonious balance amongst all living patrons on earth. This gave further meaning to the importance of my angelic work.

"When you began to write to me it became abundantly clear you had overcome everything that had been thrown at you. I must say, I very much enjoyed those letters. That and your everyday actions is how I knew you were ready and it was only a matter of time until our long entwined journey would end. I know your wish won't be squandered, and you know what Pop? I can now leave this place. I can go home and see Mary. She's waiting for me. She took her last breath only a few hours ago! That's why I am here now. I could have gone a long time ago, but I wanted to wait. I wanted to meet her at home so we can travel together, the way we always used to."

"Drewford is this real?" I asked.

"This is the realest it will ever be, Pop."

With that, an announcement squawked over the tinny station tannoy:

The 6.15 train to Poughkeepsie is about to depart, all aboard, all aboard!

"That's my cue Pop. It's finally time to go home to see my Mary."

Drewford stood up and gave me a strong and firm handshake. But that was little too impersonal, and I went in for an almighty hug wrapping my arms around him, bear hug style.

Tears ran down my face, the emotions impossible to hold back from the enormity of it all.

Our journey together had been immense, my tears were of joy not sadness.

Drewford knew this and smiled, he handed me a handkerchief from the inside pocket of his dashing navy tweed blazer.

"Don't worry I've got two. I am going to need one when I see Mary," he said with a cheeky wink, one I'd seen before. It was somehow identical to Mary's.

"Don't stop writing your diaries Pop, one day they might help someone else the same way my words helped you."

It was right then I realised I had so much more I wanted to ask Drew, and in the heat of the moment I asked,

"Drewford what about the dream of you and Mary on the train. Why did you want me to turn your book into an album?"

Drewford smiled wide.

"That was all you Pop. You always had it in you, you just needed a vehicle to take you there, that was all on you, my friend."

I responded with another audible gasp, too many to count at this point.

"It goes back to why I picked you in the first place Pop,

What did my Mary say? Ahhh yes. You can see things for what they could be, not necessarily for what they really are. Something along those lines wasn't it?

"You used my book as an excuse to be your own band, a reason to make your own music. This was just your own internal instinct rejuvenating your once dormant creative spirit. It's like that completely coincidental small black bird that sparked your first moment of curiosity and enlightened your imagination and sense of wonder as a child. That was all on you Pop, your Grandpa was right when he nicknamed you Wonderboy! Pop I must say, I am flattered you found so much inspiration from me and my notepad, I enjoy your music very much, The Life & Times of Drewford Alabama. Gee, what a world!"

As he walked off, he was gently humming the melody to one of the songs on the album, a track called 'Water.' Then he stopped to turn round.

"What a great singer that chap is. Something Dangerfield right?"

"Right," I said wiping tears from my damp face.

"One last thing," he shouted. "It's been a pleasure to watch you bang those drums Pop Morrison, your gift brings a lot of people joy, the best is yet to come though. The best is yet to come."

As I was about to respond, my viewpoint suddenly changed. I was now hovering above Drewford as he got on the Poughkeepsie train for the final time. He had somehow procured a bunch of white Alabaster roses which sat on the seat beside him in the empty carriage. The journey zipped across the landscape and within seconds he arrived at Poughkeepsie station where he hurriedly disembarked the locomotive for the short walk home to his dear beloved Mary.

Within moments, Drewford turned the corner and arrived at his picturesque white house with its baby blue trim and immaculate floral garden. He waited at the picket gate for Mary, just like they did as childhood sweethearts, then adults, and now in death. Seconds later, she appeared at the door. Her face light up as she walked down the pristine pathway of their gorgeous home. As she reached the gate Drewford ever the gentleman held it open for Mary to walk through, straight into his arms, an embrace over forty years in the making.

They held each other in a way that's reserved only for the truest of loves. Mary touched Drewford's face, and he smiled a smile I know he had been waiting a very long time to deliver.

Drewford put his hands on Mary's small waist and whispered softly into her ear, "I am so sorry I am late, my love. I got held up."

Mary, holding his face with both hands, said with tenderness,

"I understand Drew. Now we will never be apart again."

The couple walked into the Poughkeepsie sunset holding hands, trading stories, and laughing, finally together again, only this time forever.

I wanted to go with them, but I was suspended in the air watching.

I noticed they were wearing matching clothes, his and hers navy blue tweed suits.

There they went, twinned, tweed, love birds finally set free. This moment deserved a round of applause. I clapped vigorously, gaining the attention of the two Alabamas who both turned around. They waved back, their faces lit up with an all-encompassing peace, the true meaning of 'rest in peace,' both of their smiles saying a thousand words, the moment singing a thousand songs. Without taking my eyes off the couple I was sure Drewford was moments away from shouting one last message to me, of who knows what possibilities. And, as I braced to listen, everything went black.

When I woke up from this dream, I had been crying, my face puffy and the pillow wet with tears. I wanted to see Tutti, so I got myself together quickly and headed downstairs. The second I saw her I held her close and told her how much I loved her.

Then I suggested we should start wearing matching clothes.

"Are you alright sweetie?" she asked while pulling free the handkerchief hanging from my pyjama shirt pocket.

"Yes, yes, I really am," I said confidently.

Dabbing my damp eyes, she asked where the elegant hanky came from,

"A friend I once knew. I promise to tell you about him one day," I said continuing to hold her tight.

The year – 2012

Date – August 12th

Time – 2.45pm

Location – London

Three weeks had passed scene my angelic Alabama dream.

Like most days, the sound of Roscoe scratching at the bedroom door had woken me up. The scratching meant he wanted his morning walkie. If he barked that would indicate he was hungry, kinda like me in a way.

With Roscoe's comfort break at the top of my priorities I threw on my sparkly green tracksuit and standard issue morning sunglasses and headed out to the grassy part inside of Soho Square. There's a little coffee hut called "The Magic Spoon" by a broken water fountain which makes a mean macchiato, the Spanish owner Gabriella is rather fond of Roscoe and always comes out from behind the counter to deliver my frothy caffeinated drink.

Roscoe adored Gabriella as she always had a treat for him. That day he got his absolute favourite, a day-old muffin.

Cloud nine.

Talking about clouds, the sky was chock-full with Grandpa's favourite skyward spectacle the good old, 'good luck' Cirrus cloud. I had never seen so many of the angelic skyward treats. I imagined Grandpa would have said something like, *There's fortune as far the eye can see.* That or something better.

When we got home, I sat on the terrace under the gorgeous Cirrus blanket with the buzz of London contemporaneously mixing in with Ludwig van Beethoven's *Moonlight Sonata* playing on the small pink radio inside the flat.

The classical music station *Classic Radio* was, and still is a standard musical morning feature at our place. Roscoe absolutely loves it.

Tutti left for her job in the City early and pretty much always tuned in whilst having her morning toast and chocolate milk. Every so often she opted for silence, the latter scenario always resulting with me later finding Roscoe in the kitchen staring longingly up at the radio, his head adorably cocked to the side giving off a faint symphonic sympathy-inducing whimper.

So there I was sitting on the terrace, acclimatising to the new day, as Ludwig van's piano masterpiece concluded, I was sufficiently awake to check the news.

I turned on my laptop and began the usual rounds of sites I routinely visit, none of which would be deemed, *standard news*. My go-tos all being music, fashion or art related.

The first headline on 'Everything Music dot com' floored me.

The Valentines' drummer quits band

One of my all-time favourite bands just lost their long time drummer on the eve of a colossal tour. This rarely happens to the big bands, smaller bands certainly so, but the big ones, hardly ever.

Mega big bands operate much more like the mafia.

You're in it for life or until you die.

I called Tutti Frutti straight away.

"Tutti you see the link I just sent?"

Clearly not, as moments later, her "No way" sounded like a fresh surprise to me.

"It's going to be mine Tutti," I said firmly.

My inner confidence was back.

It felt like I had a stack of winning lottery tickets in my back pocket. Presumptuous, I know, but it wasn't as simple as just wanting this opportunity, it wasn't even as simple as believing in angels or wishes. Deep down I knew there was no more perfect human out there for this prestigious position, I hadn't just been a fan of The Valentines – I spent my formative years at the local youth club playing bad cover versions of their songs with my equally unskilled friends. We were kids but the music was already flowing through me.

The difference now was that I was a serious drummer. I could play with a spirit and energy required to give the music the justice it deserved.

"What you doing talking to me then sweetheart? Make some calls!"
Tutti was right; she's always right.

A quick 'love you babe,' sign off and I did exactly that, trying to connect the musical dots, so to speak.

It all came together very quickly without obstacle or friction and within the hour I was in touch with Joey Valentine the lead singer and overall mastermind of the group. Joey and I were fast exchanging text messages I was invited to the band's West London studio for what he described as a 'kick about'. The list of five songs that followed the invitation would later raise a giggle as my cocky response was Joey's first clue that I was the right man for the job.

"I know these songs already mate!"

A week later I was asked to fill the abandoned drum throne for the upcoming sold out enormodome tour. The manager called me a few days before it all began, to tell me not to get too excited as the shows should be treated like an exam, his exact words, "The end results will determine the end result. Good luck."

Managers in the music business are cold folk. His 'good luck' had its own essence of sarcasm, you just had to know what to look out for: this wasn't my first rodeo. I flushed the BS where it belonged. I was experienced enough to know this test wasn't all about music or ability. I was all too aware you need more strings on your bow than just talent, that will only ever take you half-way there, what you really need is that figurative coat of armour that only real life experience will ever give you, CHECK. I'd had myself a healthy dose of that, you could now say I was the full package.

It was like a butterfly effect of past experiences and hard to comprehend scenarios had brought me to this point and in the blink of an eye I was back out on the road tearing up the stages.

My presence fit like a glove and every musician, including myself, had the time of our lives on stage every night. That was the biggest conformation you could ever have, undeniable really does carry a definitive vibe.

The band asked me to join the group properly just before we went out to play the encore on the last show of the tour. Once we wrapped up our performance, I walked off stage, in the corner of my eye I saw the manager waiting in the wings, and I made a beeline for him.

Exhilarated and dripping with sweat, I asked him, "How did I do?"

"Welcome to the family Pop."

It was once again musical La familia – for the second time in my life.

I'd been given a second chance and this time round I knew exactly what to do with it. I guess I did end up joining an army. I now travel the world with an army of brothers, the weapons being loud drums and guitars.

Drewford was right when he said, "The best was yet to come."

I was back in a band where I belonged, and it never felt better. I was making albums, touring the world, shooting videos, and winning awards. Life was peachy swell and the years started to tick by gracefully like the hands working their elegant way around that famous Grand Central Station clock.

Tutti and I bought our first home together. This wasn't just any home. This was a fairytale house most fitting for our fairytale love. The Californian weed shares I bought one drunken night way back when were now worth an astronomical sum of money. We decided to cash in and only a few weeks later bought a little country house hidden behind dramatic silver birch and monkey puzzle trees, nestled between the hilly green Hertfordshire-Surrey borders. We loved London and our kooky Denmark Street bolt hole, but when Mr Kinsey sold the building, it coincided with our mega cash breakthrough. It wasn't a hard decision to pack it all up and head to the sticks.

London and The Morrisons had to part ways.

We had *been there, got the T-shirt*.

A new home was required and '*the manor*' was just that.

You could get lost there, and when we first moved in, I often did. One day I found myself in the attic curiously rummaging around some of our yet-to-be unboxed up sentimental items. This is where I got reacquainted with my old diaries, they were in a dusty cardboard box next to a large faded wooden rocking horse that one of the previous owners of the house had left behind.

I couldn't not give it a whirl, could I?

Sitting up on that wooden horse whilst covered in coloured light from the two circular stained-glass windows at either end of the attic roof I began reading.

Going through the diaries, combined with my vivid memories of those shiny bright peaks and moody dark troughs, I realised that words really can't express happiness and sadness in their truest sense. There's a subtlety to these feelings that is simply indescribable – probably a good thing. Some stuff must be left to experience, it can't be learnt in a book, movie or your friends' advice. Only 'experiencing' brings the truest sense of any sentiment.

Now I have one last morsel of this story to share with you before we say goodbye.

Everyone's heard these sayings.

History has a habit of repeating itself.
Or
What goes around comes around.

When I went and left my class act of a briefcase in the back of a taxi, life really did repeat itself and history certainly came back to say hello.

I was coming home from a night out with guys in the band, *the gang.*

We had been at a dry private members club in Chiswick an enclave of London that is more akin to a village than your typical citified image of London. High tax bracket residents only here, folks.

As I no longer drank alcohol, social situations at this point in my life relied solely on the quality of the companionship. The current tipple of choice was my old 'go to' Gin and tonic minus the gin and instead of tonic, sparkling water with lots and lots of ICE. Four beers and a fizzy water were the continuous orders at the bar.

This evening and all the way into the wee hours of the morning I heard stories of past hilarity, successes, losses, heartbreaks, and musical adventure. It was clear that this was the rock and roll elite, a club where I had somehow found myself slap bang in the middle.

I was consumed, immersed, and fully inspired.

A heady trio indeed.

Getting home way past four, I was unaware of what I had left behind in the back of the cab. I only realised the next day when I went to write in my diary which I kept in the briefcase's secret compartment.

History had repeated itself.

The lost diary contained my mind's inner workings, my thoughts about getting a second bite of that golden delicious apple or things of that nature. I can't remember what was in there. All I know is that it was all from the heart.

That apple by the way, is so much sweeter the second time around, I can tell you that!

When I realised what a blunder I'd made, I knew I would never see the briefcase or diary again.

I imagined that Drewford knew how this would play out... What am I saying, of course he knew!

I called all the Chiswick cab companies to no avail. I figured whoever was in the car after me thought they could make a couple of quid out of it, after all that briefcase was a class act. I didn't, and still don't mind one bit. I hope it ends up in a thrift store somewhere.

I hope that my words will be found by someone who at some point will need them just as much as I needed Drewford Alabama's.

History was coming full circle.

The Wonderboy's fit to burst diary out there somewhere, completely lost, waiting to be found. I like that thought very much. So, with that said I think it's time for me to call our last moments together.

THE END

Acknowledgements

Thank you to all my band mates past and present, Laura Dockrill, the team at Seren, FMcM, Judy Parkinson, Pete Fowler, Sam Semple and Claire Scott.

The Author

Jamie Morrison is a British musician songwriter and producer, best known as the drummer in the Welsh band Stereophonics. In his teens, he formed the band Noisettes and had world-wide success. Since 2017 he has been part of a new project called 86TVs, featuring The Maccabees siblings Hugo, Felix and Will White. They signed to Parlophone records in 2022.

He has recently turned to writing and has been prolific penning over 100 short stories. In addition to his debut novel. He is a keen chef, gardener, lover of animals, aspiring pilot.